TWO ON THE
RIVER

The Atlantic Monthly Press
Boston · New York

TWO ON THE
RIVER

WIL HAYGOOD

Photography by
STAN GROSSFELD

First Edition

This book is an expanded version of an article that appeared originally in the *Boston Globe Magazine*. The author and photographer wish to thank the *Globe* for permission to reprint that material.

The photo on pages 50–51 appears courtesy of the *Mark Twain Memorial*, Hartford, Connecticut.

Published simultaneously in Canada

Design by Dianne Schaefer *Design*
Typesetting by DEKR Corporation
Printed in Japan by Dai Nippon Printing Company

For my family

W.H.

TWO ON THE RIVER

At night a glow would lie over the river, and the river seemed to bleed something soft and black that settled around and enabled you to rock with nature, to hum. The glow was moonlight, and the only sounds came from crickets singing against the air, trees rustling night toward morning, and the hum in your throat. The banks of the river were mere shadows, and in the shadows lay the secrets of the old river.

Spend six weeks on the Mississippi River; travel the roads of Iowa and Wisconsin and Kentucky where they stretch along the river. Make your way to Hannibal, Missouri, where boys along the riverbank are Huck Finning their way through life, and you may begin to feel the secrets of the river loosen.

Continue for more than three hundred miles on a raft and you learn that the raft does not belong to you but to the river and the power of storms. The raft can carry you where you've never been before, into river towns and into the souls of river people who come down to the bank to welcome you as if they knew, before you did, that one day you would wash up to their land and lay the palm of your hand against theirs.

Go into the Deep South on a steamboat and see how the land and river and wind change. Sit beside a steamboat captain at one o'clock in the morning as he steers his boat down the Mississippi, through rising fog and around the bends. Spend time on the river with the fishermen and oilmen who live a life as unpredictable as a throw of the dice. Talk to river men older than this century who sit in the Arkansas and Mississippi shade and still dream the soft dreams of poets and still have stories to tell.

Drift at last into Pilottown, an island of Louisiana that sits on stilts in the Mississippi, just at the lip of the Gulf of Mexico, and talk with river pilots who look out at the water and wait for their ships to come in from ports around the world.

When you do this, you begin to bump up against history. You begin to understand why the story of Mark Twain and the Mississippi River, seventy-five years after his death and one hundred years after he published a book about a boy named Huck and a slave named Jim that seems not to have been written but to have pulsed out of the very land and water, continues to beat against the soul of humanity with a permanence all its own.

The 2,550-mile journey began for the two of us on an April afternoon on Lake Itasca in northern Minnesota. We hiked a quarter mile and saw the land opening onto the lake. Another quarter mile and we were at the foot of the lake; we didn't have to look at the wooden sign jammed right there into the earth to know that we had reached the headwaters of the Mississippi River. We could feel it. The air was cool and clean. Water begot

East Hannibal, Illinois

water: the lake rushed over the slick backs of rocks that lay in the water, and that was how Lake Itasca turned into the Mississippi. Henry Schoolcraft was the first to find these headwaters, in 1832.

On that day in April 1985 a man in a big Stetson hat emerged from behind the birch trees, leaning on a cane and walking with the melancholy gait of an explorer. Two women appeared over his left shoulder, walking slowly, as if pulled by an invisible rope attached to the man's waist. He introduced himself — Dick Swanson, from Park Rapids, Minnesota.

Broad-chested Dick Swanson used to run a service business for trailers until a kidney went bad, forcing him to retire. One of the women, Geneva, was his wife. The other, Beulah Pierson, was a relative, a seventy-year-old cattle rancher from Texas. The Swansons had brought her to the river because she had never been close enough to the Mississippi to touch it — to have it touch her.

Geneva Swanson inched her way to the water and dropped her feet in, then screamed through the air at her sister-in-law: "Beulah, you get over here and put your feet in the *Mississippi River*."

Beulah Pierson, all lady and all Texas, said there was no way she was going to take her shoes off and put her feet in the Mississippi River. She knelt and dipped her blue-veined hands in the water and let it go at that. Dick Swanson smiled underneath his Stetson, and the smile fell into the shadow of his body at his feet. They all walked back up along the road and disappeared behind the birch trees, which rose high and made them look as small as puppets.

Lake Itasca, Minnesota

Then we took our shoes off, rolled up our pants, and started to walk across the river, ten feet wide, three feet deep, and freezing cold. As we approached the halfway point, a tall and beautiful bird landed on a nearby rock and craned its neck, as if to mock. We reached the other side, stood a few moments shivering on the bank, then crossed back over.

"Now," Stan said, "we can tell people we walked across the Mississippi River. Legends in our own time."

The tall, beautiful bird arose from the rock, and, for a few moments, was stilled, fluttering in one spot, as if figuring in which direction to go. It finally soared toward the west and vanished under the gleam of white-yellow sunlight.

The river curved and kept curving here, around birch and pine trees that were not quite full of green yet. Patches of harmless snow dotted the land.

We drove downriver a mile or so, got out of the car, and started walking down a steep hill. Before we reached the bottom of the hill, I knelt and picked a daisy and placed it in the band of my straw hat. We walked over to a bit of land that sloped off toward the river. The ground was cold because the sun had not

Lake Itasca, Minnesota

broken through the trees to warm it. Gray stones rose from the ground. It was a little cemetery, and the way it was hidden, I figured it was private. One of the stones said AMY JILSON: 1912–1912. A biography over before it began. That burial day in 1912 must have seemed, for the parents, to exist for no other reason than sadness.

A tiny American flag flapped on the side of another stone, which sat inside a small fence. Through the layer of trees the river looked to be a metallic blue. As we climbed the hill returning to the car, the wind blew the daisy from my hat, and I watched it float until I lost sight of it.

We took to the road again, passing quiet land flat as a football field where homes sat in the distance. Our eyes went beyond the homes into more distance.

We stopped for lunch at a diner right off the road. While the waitress served tuna and french fries, I asked, "What happens around here at night?"

"What you into, rock or metal?"

"Neither."

"Can't help you then."

We paid and drove on and met Dan, our pilot, for our return flight to St. Paul. He had flown us from there to Bemidji — twenty miles below the headwaters. Dan did little talking: from North Dakota, married, a father, been flying "a long time."

The Cessna Skyhawk lifted off the runway nicely. Soon we were over the river, which looked like a brown snake. Thirty minutes in the air, the plane started rocking hard and a rainstorm battered the windows. Stan gave me an oh-hell glance and I returned it. Dan didn't flinch, just worked the dials and said, "Don't worry." He glided the plane over the Mississippi River and landed it on a strip of St. Paul airfield. An old pro, a day at the office. He walked from the plane steady as a soldier. We walked as if we had been punched.

The gold horses atop the 1840-built capitol in St. Paul looked new and gallant, especially at night, when they were silhouetted against a quiet blue-black sky.

Tycoons gave this city its life, and many of them lived in the Victorian homes along Summit and Grand avenues. Those streets are still bordered with the large, elegant homes, fronted by lawns big enough for croquet games.

Edward and Mollie Fitzgerald gave birth at 481 Laurel Street on September 24, 1896, to Francis Scott Key Fitzgerald; a simple "F. Scott" would do for the rest of the world.

Hastings, Minnesota

Near Bemidji, Minnesota

On a late afternoon, I went over to the house where Fitzgerald would live later in life, 599 Summit Avenue, and stood on the walkway that split the lawn. A small gold-plated sign hung above the doorway, put there by the National Historic Register.

He was thin and blond and given to poetic asides. He made no academic impression at St. Paul Academy, so in the fall of 1911, F. Scott Fitzgerald was sent east, to the Newman School in Hackensack, New Jersey. After prep school, he entered Princeton University, where he walked the campus swinging a walking stick. The old-club charm of the school seduced him.

At Princeton he found his writing voice, romantic and lyrical. He drank, first socially, then almost consistently, and to some was already an alcoholic before the calendar went from his freshman to his sophomore year.

Before his senior year he went off to war — really just down to a military base outside Montgomery, Alabama. He wore tailor-made Brooks Brothers army outfits and took notes as if he were a documentary filmmaker, already rummaging out of his personal life incidents that would end up in his short stories and novels.

At a dance in Montgomery, on a July night in 1918, he met a young woman named Zelda Sayre, who told him, shortly after their meeting, that she did not want to end up in life as "Miss Alabama Nobody." They had a romance. He proposed and she said no and he returned to St. Paul to write his first novel, *This Side of Paradise*. His novel was published and generally praised by the critics. His star began to move, and Zelda drifted to him like a moth to light.

They married in New York City and became a part of the shenanigans of the Jazz Age: staying out all night, riding on the tops of cars, being thrown out of hotels, drinking gin as if it were water. As he himself put it, "Finding no nucleus to which we could cling, we became a small nucleus ourselves and gradually we fitted our disruptive personalities into the contemporary scene of New York."

In France they danced on the Riviera, ate meals with Hemingway, tried to figure out his psyche behind his back.

Another book, *The Beautiful and Damned*, was published. They thought they'd be perfect as the leading man and lady, but neither ever made it to the screen.

Back in America, Zelda battled mental illness, and F. Scott's own health began to fail from his excessive drinking. Still, the pull at each other's heart was known to be almost uncanny. The books were dedicated to her: "To Zelda," "Once Again to Zelda."

He rarely returned to St. Paul, complaining that the winters there were too unromantic.

The Great Gatsby, about a young man who leaves Minnesota and changes his name and becomes rich and falls in love with a woman named Daisy, may be his best book. Fame came to him fast, left even faster. F. Scott wondered, though, if *The Great Gatsby* would last.

Broke, an alcoholic, and on the ropes, he went to Hollywood to write movie scripts. Hollywood was not the place to go when on the ropes. They butchered his scripts and he complained. He sulked and had his first heart attack on Sunset Boulevard. A few days later, alone in his apartment, he had another heart attack, this one fatal.

Zelda, in a letter, remembered the night they met. "It was a radiant night, a night of soft conspiracy and the trees agreed that it was all going to be for the best."

She died in a fire in a mental hospital, burned beyond recognition, on March 10, 1948.

"I am not a great man," Fitzgerald once said, "but sometimes I think the impersonal and objective quality of my talent, and the sacrifices of it, in pieces, to preserve its essential value, has some sort of epic grandeur."

My hands had been clasped behind my back and I unclasped them and turned and walked away. The evening was cool, and now yellow lights burned behind curtains in the homes along Summit Avenue.

Minneapolis, across the river from St. Paul, had the scent of newness, with tall, shiny buildings everywhere. Yet, no matter where our eyes went in Minneapolis, we noticed knots of Indians on street corners, and there was about them the defeatist look that poverty has been known to carry with it.

Something was awry. Once, the Indians lived by the river, where they traded and told their children wise things, and the river was happiness. But time had been cruel. Men with fast ideas got the best of the Indian. A young Indian with a sad look on his face, hair drooping along his neck, asked, "Where is there to go? There's nothing on the reservations, so you leave and come here and try to find work."

At night in Minnesota, when the green land had gone both dark and dark green, the Indians who remained on the reservations beat their drums, and the echoes rose up over the hills.

On a lazy evening, Stan suggested we go swimming in the hotel pool, "to get ready for the river." It was one of those nominal hotel pools, small with a tall plant in the corner. I edged to the pool, afraid to jump, then heard a splash that was Stan, already stroking. Then I jumped in, came up fast, and swam awkwardly to the nearest edge: I'm no smooth swimmer. Stan looked at me in silence, then cut the silence by saying, "You better not

fall in that river. We'll be in deep trouble." His words stuck like darts. We hit the steam room for twenty minutes and mumbled forgettable words about the need to be ready.

Later that night on the hotel balcony, which looked out onto the river, black as ink in the night, we uncorked champagne. "Here's to the journey, and the Mississippi River." There was the clink of champagne glasses. Stan raised his arm, cocked it back, and threw the cork out toward the river, imagining that the night wind would take it and place it in the current. "We'll catch up with the cork in St. Louis," he said, and before the last word had gotten out, the cork had disappeared.

The next day we went to Eddie Bauer, a sporting goods store, and bought supplies. We reeled off a list of items, and the young salesman hustled down the aisles. Sleeping bags. Cooking gear. Rope. Flashlights.

"Give us the best," Stan yelled down one of the aisles.

"Hey, we better watch the budget," I said. Stan inched closer. "Listen, we don't want to get out there on that river and die because of cheap equipment." We loaded the supplies into the trunk and drove through thick noontime traffic to find the road by the river, letting it take us.

The northern river is a different river from the southern river. Mark Twain was not as close to it as to the southern portion, which he lived by and navigated. He considered it halfhearted for people to talk about "knowing" the Mississippi without traveling its entire length, so he journeyed several times upriver during his lifetime so that that part of the river could color his soul and, perhaps, teach him things.

In 1895 a lecturing Twain, then sixty years old, sold out the Minneapolis Opera House. A critic described his lecturing style: "He starts off in a funny little jog trot, half sideways, with his eyes cast up to the gallery, with a comical look of half inquiry and half appeal. Then he begins to deliver his humorous conceits with an expression of placid child-like innocence that is almost as ludicrous as the words he is uttering."

Minnesota never saw Mark Twain again after 1895, though he lived for fifteen more years.

By noon the next day we were rolling along a road that led us into Red Wing, Minnesota, a town carved out of limestone bluffs. The bluffs, ragged and brown, looked down on Main Street as if to keep an eye on all the goings-on.

When river pilots anchored in Red Wing they would take a room at the elegant St. James Hotel, built in 1875 by a group of

Near Winona, Minnesota

investors in town, men like Jesse McIntire and Joshua Pierce, money men with grand ideas. The St. James, situated on the west bank of the river, was distinguished by the balconies that stretched around the hotel. Gentlemen whispered to ladies on those balconies and watched the sun set. But the years worked hard on the elegance and tradition, and not ten years ago the St. James was sitting silent, a flophouse ready for the wrecking ball. Then someone put two and two together and figured the hotel could be restored to its earlier splendor.

A black Steinway, built in 1887, sat in the all-wood, antique-filled lobby of the restored St. James. The easy light of chandeliers draped the dining room, where silver lay atop white cotton tablecloths, where the windows gave a view of the Mississippi.

Memories of the riverboat era hung gloomily over Red Wing. In July of 1890 the big steamer *Sea Wing* left town and never came back. The captain was caught in fog, the boat capsized, and forty people from Red Wing died. They closed the town for four days and mourned. Town residents would go out to the banks of the river to see if the bodies of relatives or friends had washed onto land. When patience wore thin and bodies were still missing, dynamite was thrown into the river to bring more bodies to the surface.

Cry a little more for Red Wing. Back in 1940 a storm started on the river and four men from town were out there, stranded. A young lawyer named Arnie Vogel, who knew the river, gathered three of his buddies and the four of them went looking for the men. Their wives wanted to stop them at the door but didn't.

Vogel still lives in Red Wing, still remembers: "There was so much fog out there, and it was cold too. We made it to a little island where we saw that the boat had capsized." They found all four men, but none of them had a breath of life left. They were frozen to death. Arnie Vogel and his buddies made *Life* magazine: a little story and picture about the rescue attempt.

Arnie Vogel was eighty now, still with his wife, Marjorie, whom he'd married more than forty years before. Just recently he had hired a man to help him tend his land. Arnie Vogel would still love to work the land with his own hands. The mind was willing; it was the body that had shifted gears.

A Sunday afternoon was passing and Vogel said, "Think I'm gonna go out, gonna take the wife and go upriver." He'd gotten his boat from his father-in-law as a wedding gift, and after all these years, Arnie and Marjorie still had a romance, and a river to travel on in the softness of an afternoon.

The bluffs of Red Wing followed us out of town, past farmhouses and wheat fields that leaned with the wind under a bone-white sky.

Winona, Minnesota

It was high noon at the Mississippi Belle Restaurant in Hastings, Minnesota. Tom Olson, the restaurant manager, stood on a stool cleaning the hanging light bulbs that lit the restaurant his grandfather had founded. His brocade vest glittered in the light that fell upon it. A pair of bifocals hung from his neck on a piece of string.

"We've been trying to revitalize," he said, when asked about the quiet of the town. There were two others inside the restaurant: the lunch crowd. "We don't have the old riverboats anymore. The railways came and the river died." The way he said it, low in the throat, one would have thought they had had a funeral and all for the river.

We ordered steaks and fries and sipped cola from tall red glasses. There were no windows in the restaurant, which glowed orange and saloon-red. An old Wanted poster REWARD FOR ASSASSIN OF PRESIDENT LINCOLN hung above the bar, which a waitress leaned on, counting last night's receipts.

Years ago, Olson explained, men used to bootleg whiskey and liquor out of the restaurant. They'd hustle up off a riverboat, buy the booze, make back for the river, and float away.

A waitress bounced by and said, "We got fresh pies." Then Olson said, hooking onto her words, "Got a lady lives on the outskirts of town, makes 'em for us, brings 'em right in from her kitchen." The lemon pie was delicious, and I said to myself, whatever they paid the lady who lived on the outskirts of town, it wasn't enough.

We wanted to buy the cook a drink. "He stopped drinking a few years back," Olson said, and that settled that.

We got up and walked through the redness of the restaurant out the door, and stood for a few moments readjusting our eyes to the brittle sunlight. Then we went around the side of the restaurant and down to the river. It flowed smooth and easy. We spread out five feet from each other and began skipping rocks across the river, watching them disappear under the surface. Stan's rocks went the farthest, and I began cocking my arm back farther, watching him out the corner of my eye to see if he had some little trick with the wrist. There was no trick: apparently it was just skill. Twenty quiet and beautiful minutes passed with the only movement the skipping rocks that sent rings across a small portion of the river. Stan was declared the winner. We turned our backs to the river and walked to the car and rode until the lights of day went out. Lightning bugs flicked across the land, like miniature bulbs.

Tom Olson, Hastings, Minnesota

Earth softened, flowers grew, birds sang, air warmed, smiles increased, roads opened wide. The surface of America fluttered in an early spring. The green seemed to come at us, to crawl up our arms and then around our shoulders, to put us at ease.

Bridges rose up and stretched across the Mississippi River, which separated state from state. Such a bridge showed the way from Minnesota into Prescott, Wisconsin, where old buildings leaned into the street and people walked in and out of their shade. The sun spread across the town with the gentleness of a big hand on your back: not a strange hand, but the kind of warm hand you had felt before.

A man sat on the steps at the side of the hardware store, smoking a cigarette. The cigarette smoke curled up and over his left shoulder. I walked up to him, tried making conversation about the town, the river. His face was unshaven and his eyes were tired. He offered a few words, then stopped, rolled his words back up, and confessed that neither the town nor the river had ever meant much to him. The cigarette in his hand was short now, and he brought it up to his lips, Bogart-like, and stared across the street at nothing in particular. It was that kind of dead stare that said: Go away, buddy. I turned, then heard the man say, "You wanna know about the river, see Captain Beeler. Lives up the hill."

The road wound up and around, as if on a slow-motion spin. Railroad tracks were down below a ledge and at the bottom of the ledge lay the river. Homes were tucked back from trees. Screen doors opened and shut. Garments flapped on clotheslines. Folks sat on porches in swings, eyed the car, waved.

Mrs. Beeler came to the door, one pink hand on the screen door, another on her apron. She yelled over her shoulder, "Honey, there's someone here who wants to talk to you about the river." As we stepped inside the well-decorated home, a mirror threw our reflection back at us. Before we got to the living room Captain Robert Beeler was up, making his way slowly down into the basement, as if he had anticipated this meeting for the longest time.

"Come on down here," he said, flicking a big arm out, guiding, not even asking to see press credentials.

He was sixty-eight years old and dressed easy enough for Sunday-morning golf. His life had been lived by the light of the river. Now the captain had Parkinson's disease and was just coming off an operation. He moved as if negotiating a swinging bridge. The grace was in the eyes now. And if you sat and listened to his story, you forgot about the Parkinson's and realized you were talking to a man who was once the happiest man on

The riverbank

the river, a twenty-one-year-old captain who took big boats downstream.

We were in the cool basement where the stilled part of the captain's life rested. The river itself was reflected in the mirror above the bar. Pictures of steamboats, black-and-white photos and a few color paintings, hung everywhere, on all walls in both rooms of the basement. There were more than three hundred pictures. "I got more to frame yet," he said. These were the steamboats that people in the river towns once lined the banks to wave at. "All these new boats I don't give a darn for," he said.

In one corner of the basement, frozen in a lovely wood frame, was a picture of the *Mark Twain*. She once went up and down the river with Captain Robert Beeler at the wheel. That would have been during the 1950s, when he was young, out in front of the years, bringing boats through morning fog.

He told how he got pulled down to the river. "I was seventeen, just got out of school, and heard that the *Dakota* was looking for a couple of men." He started at the bottom, scrubbing the deck, moving equipment, making forty-two bucks a month, a fortune for a young man doing the only thing he ever wanted to do. The good ones got noticed, were heard like voices on an empty stage. A captain took the young Beeler under his wing, groomed him, taught him to read the river the way a surveyor reads the land. "And once you get your feet wet in the river, you're gone," he said.

There are eastern universities that now grant maritime degrees, and a part of the degree is supposed to qualify you to be a steamboat captain. When Beeler was coming up you didn't need a degree to ride the river. "You got to run over the river to know it," said the man who should know. "I got fifty years of my life in the river." Yet, the era he knew and lived was pretty much over, and only the faint music of the steamboat whistle was left.

The steamboat era grew old when it was still young. Some of the boats shown on Captain Beeler's basement walls died when their time was just beginning to pass. The companies that owned the boats no longer had use for them, so company workmen took them out to the middle of the river, poured gasoline on their decks, struck a match, and watched them burn. The collapsed wood floated downriver and that was the epitaph.

Captain Robert Beeler cannot ride the river now and he may never get back out there. So he had a chair in his living room, right by the window that looked out onto the river. Beside the chair he kept a stand with a pair of binoculars and a maritime radio. He knew the boats that went by, had their schedules worked out in his mind, and would grab his radio and hold a little conversation with a passing captain. When it got dark and

the moonlight lying on the river was not bright enough to help him make out a passing boat, he would go for his big blinker and send a blinking message, and when a blinking message was sent back through the moonlight, an old river captain felt young again.

A few years back, President Jimmy Carter, aboard the *Delta Queen,* came down the Mississippi River, right by the captain's window. The captain, on the edge of his chair, blinked a message to the *Delta Queen*. No one answered. The Secret Service guys on board probably thought it was some wise guy. Nope, just Captain Robert Beeler.

He was married in 1941. Evelyn, his wife, knew what kind of life it would be: her husband away for days, sometimes for weeks at a time. But sometimes she'd pack up, a spur of the moment thing, and go meet the captain at a river town, a long good-bye followed by a surprising hello.

"The boats used to be so, well, *dignified*," she said. "Now they got captains who wear T-shirts." The captain who never wore a T-shirt shook his head.

A good day wore on, and the captain, sensing we'd have to be moving along, said, "If you got one more minute, I got something I'd like to show you." He and his wife moved in perfect harmony toward the closet. They brought out leather-bound albums filled with newspaper clippings and pictures. There it was: the captain once ran for mayor. Lost by a few votes. The captain and Evelyn threw their heads back and laughed at it. Heck, he was a river man, not a politician. And they showed some pictures of the captain, young and spiffied up in captain's suit, smiling, the jaw jutting, the eyes slits of light.

"It was a good life," the captain said. "I sent four kids to college. Built a nice home. Got a few bucks in the bank. Yep, the river done all right by me." He raised an arm and rested it around his wife's waist.

Evelyn Beeler picked out the spot for their house because she knew her husband needed the river. If no one else knew, she knew. "Come back anytime," the captain said. "The coffee's always hot."

We waved at Evelyn Beeler, who stood at the screen door, standing there for herself and her husband, who was a little tired and back in the chair in front of the window that was in front of the river. Soon, the sun began its descent and lent a violet color to the sky. We rolled through the dark, pulled into a roadside motel in the middle of nowhere, ate cheeseburgers, and called it a night.

Delta Queen ***from the*** **Mississippi Queen**

Morning came soft as a veil falling down a smooth face — sunshine, the sounds of birds, six-thirty and out on the road. An hour got lost in time, and a four-lane road led into La Crescent, Minnesota. We drove up a road that rose over our backs and showed the rooftops of the town. On the side of the road, bees buzzed in trees. The wind blew but not enough to bother. A man in a white safari hat stood on the hillside with his hands in the pockets of his money-green jump-suit. The smell of apples was everywhere. When Stan turned the car engine off, the man in the white safari hat came over and introduced himself as Louis Lautz. His skin was well lined and looked leathery.

La Crosse, Wisconsin

Lautz's ancestors had come from Germany looking for opportunity and a little land. They found both, and rode out the Depression on profits from apples that were first planted here in 1929. Before they got into apples they made a living by carving ice from the Mississippi River, which was at the bottom of the orchard hill, down where Louis Lautz's eyes had strayed: "Carved big chunks of ice out of that river."

There was a red barn in which to store apples, and apple wood was stacked high as our waist by the side of the barn. When Louis Lautz and his wife, Bonnie, sat at home, with winter roaring outside, he said that they would throw some apple wood into the fireplace, and soon they'd be right back in the apple orchard.

The apples were picked every year by college students and by migrant workers, who move with the seasons. They just came up over the hill, asked for buckets, and started picking, Lautz said. They brought canteens and sleeping bags and slept with the stars on their eyelids.

"I like the loneliness of being up here," he said, squinting and looking around with eyes that were green and set in deep sockets. His face was lined enough to catch shadows from the sunlight that broke through the tips of the apple trees. There were seventy acres of Lautz land.

He was born here sixty-one years ago. When he grew up, he left, trying to reach beyond the world of apple orchards. He found himself fighting in a war, flying bombers in World War II. "Some of those experiences brought me closer to God," he said. He was out over the middle of the Pacific when the atomic bomb was dropped. "They radioed me and told me to bring the plane back on home."

In 1946 he came back to Prescott. "My dad was sick. I stayed here that year, met my wife; happened to bump into her after the war. A charming gal." They had three children, and none was drawn to apple orchards the way the father was, but he was proud as can be just the same. One was a lawyer, one was a doctor, and one was a nurse.

He showed us the inside of the apple shed. It was refrigerator-cool. Equipment was scattered about. Empty bottles sat over in a corner. "We'll fill 'em with cider," he said as he headed back outside.

He did not know how the apple crop would be that year; too early to tell, even though the weather had been nice. "Looks like a good blossom, so it should be a good crop, good Lord willing." A farmer's mix of religion and the crops has never been a farfetched one.

Louis Lautz closed the door on talking because there was work to do, and the last thing we saw of him as he walked into the apple orchard was the tip of the white safari hat.

We rode down into the valley, across a bridge, and into La Crosse, Wisconsin. In the city park, ducks played and quacked on the banks of the river. An old Plymouth sat in the park, and in the front seat a guy and girl sat kissing.

Acres and acres of wheat and soybeans and corn grew in these Minnesota and Wisconsin fields. Corn grew knee-high, cattle grazed on hillsides, red barns sat in valleys, silos rose to the sky.

A boy sat on the back of a tractor while his dad drove it, and the two seemed like one, wedded to the land. In the evening, when it had grown too dark to farm, a yellow softness lay over the land and the land slept.

But seasons change and the times have been known to lean in cruel directions. The farmer was in trouble out here. Crops were not selling for what they once had because there was the problem of imports. Loans dried up. John Deere tractors were repossessed. Men in suits from banks stepped onto porches spreading news in low voices. The sweetness drained from marriages. Suicides stained the land. And worse.

In the fall of 1983 a call came through to the Buffalo Ridge State Bank, over near Ivanhoe, Minnesota. The caller said he was interested in looking at a farm and the land it was on, to appraise it all. The bank had recently repossessed the land from a father-son team, James and Steve Jenkins, who had failed to work it profitably. Deems Thulin and Rudolph Blythe went out to the Jenkins's farm to meet the caller. The rural roads were rain-slicked. The day was gray and overcast.

When the bank officers arrived they found no one interested in looking at the farm, but they did spot James and Steve Jenkins,

Overleaf: The Wisconsin River enters the Mississippi River

standing silent. Sensing trouble, the officers began to backpedal, making toward their car. The young Jenkins raised a rifle and pumped a bullet into Thulin's throat. He fell when the bullet hit. The other bank officer gasped, then quickened his pace, which turned into a trot. The young Jenkins stalked him and, when he reached him out near the road, according to court testimony, shot him dead with four bullets.

The father and son hopped into a pickup truck and gunned the engine. A passing motorist heard the commotion and gave chase as the Jenkinses sped off, firing through the window of their pickup. They disappeared, vanishing over hills and across wide-stretching roads. An all-points bulletin was flashed. Failed farmers, they were now outlaws.

Fields seemed to tighten up as tension swept across farm country. Screen doors were locked, children told to stay off the roads, to get home by dark. Farmers waded into the fields, blades of grass in between their teeth, wondering about it all. Some farmers sat in bars and leaned over beers and said it was bound to happen.

They were on the run for three days, then the boy turned himself in down in Paducah, Texas. His father was found nearby, dead, a suicide, his own gun lying across his lap.

At the trial the defense tried to put the blame on the father, saying he had an almost messianic grip over the impressionable boy, and that if the father told him to shoot someone, he would without hesitation. But the prosecutors said the father's eyesight was horrible, and painted the young Jenkins as a khaki-wearing military buff, an expert marksman who could drop a bird with one shot, a boy with a shaved head who had a grudge to beat because of the failed farm. Jurors sided with the prosecutors and young Jenkins was convicted and sentenced to seventeen years in the state prison.

Who knows what will happen when the soul is pained, when the wind at night across the farmland changes directions and dries up the ambitions that grew from the soil that yielded the crops? Passing a field and turning a corner, we saw a young kid sitting on the hood of his dad's pickup truck. He raised his hand, his forefinger poking straight up. It was a wave that said "Howdy" and "Good-bye" at the same time. He had probably seen his dad do it a thousand times.

Again, the road by the river showed the way. At the Highway Grill in Prairie du Chien, Wisconsin, Sandra Bunts suggested catfish, which we ordered because her face looked so honest. She could be your mom, standing at the end of the counter and leaning on a broom, with her sweet voice and easy manner and the plain old eyeglasses sitting on her nose.

There was, she said (beginning a story as if it came with the meal), this tugboat that came up the river last winter. It got stuck in the ice. The crew left and headed back to New Orleans, but the captain stayed behind, waiting for the ice to thaw, which would take two months. The captain sauntered about the town, becoming something of a celebrity, posing for pictures, answering questions, getting a write-up in the local paper.

"My son went down to the boat to help the captain with some chores," she said. "Then the captain had us down there for dinner. He was a southerner. He fixed shrimp jambalaya, which, you know, is real shrimp." She was staring straight out the window, still leaning on the broom.

"Well, the captain met this gal right here in town. She was a schoolteacher. He was in his fifties. He *married* the schoolteacher." With that, she leaned away from the broom. "When the river thawed the captain left, took his new bride with him. I ain't heard from him or her since, though somebody in town said they heard from her, said she's happy, living somewhere in Texas."

An idle captain. A schoolteacher. A marriage. There is hope yet for this old world.

Clinton, Iowa

I am pulled to bookstores and walked into one on the main street in Clinton, Iowa. They were all used books, and the woman behind the counter was putting some of the books into boxes. "We're going out of business," she said. "Rent's gotten too high. Got some terrific buys. Look around."

Stan strolled down one aisle and I took to another. Ten minutes later I bumped into him and saw that he had picked up a romance novel. Just as I was getting ready to scold him, he reached for Hemingway's *For Whom the Bell Tolls* and redeemed himself. I picked Fitzgerald's *The Great Gatsby,* which sold for twenty-five cents. (*The Adventures of Huckleberry Finn* was already out in the car.) The woman put the books in a brown paper bag.

We took breakfast in a little diner that glowed pink, which, I thought, was a nice touch of art deco out here in Middle America.

From a little antique shop down the street I pulled a cane from a dusty corner. Three dollars. Sold to the tall, thin man in the light-brown straw hat. (We were to take the raft at Hannibal, Missouri, and already, in the back of my mind I was imagining tools, instruments, gadgets, that would come in handy in moments of danger. So when I saw the cane I saw Stan falling from the raft and me sticking the cane out to save his life.)

We got to the red-headed woman in the parking lot before she slapped us with a ticket. Stan clicked his camera and she looked up, almost startled.

"Who the hell are you?" It was not said with malice, but nicely, even coquettishly.

"Here from Boston. Traveling the river."

"From Boston? Sure, I bet." The farther you are from home, the more suspect your story about being so far from home becomes. As the town clock struck noon we were riding under it, out of town, strangers who had just passed through.

McGregor, Iowa, looked old and weathered, as though the modern hand of time played only a minimal role in its existence. Antique stores stretched along the main street. People who passed us on the street spoke. "Hello." "Hi." "Hi ya." It was as if they knew us.

A woman inside an antique shop moved to her door. She said, pointing down the street to a large pink building that leaned over the river, "That used to be a whorehouse for all the men traveling the river. Now it's just a pink apartment building."

Farther down the street, there was a sign in the window of the River Junction Trade Company: SORRY. CLOSED FOR THE WEEK. IF SOMETHING REAL IMPORTANT CALL 873-3304. Small-town charm.

The midafternoon light showed the way up to Pike's Point in McGregor. Everything was golf-course green, and the river down below looked hazed over, smoky. A young man sat atop a rock, still as a monk, looking out over the river.

"Where's your girl?" I asked, just making talk.

"She's up the river. With another guy." I had crept up on something without wanting to.

"Sounds like a sad story," I said, feeling an urge to finish what I had started.

"Well," he said, turning his head away from the river and toward me, "that's the story of my life." Now I didn't want to continue the conversation.

We hiked up along the cool trails. Grasshoppers jumped from our path. The breeze was gentle as a bed of feathers. Every now and then we'd stop, lean against a tree, sit a spell. Stan would snap pictures and I'd try putting words down in a notebook.

We retraced our steps. Stan broke a leaf from a tree, stuck it in his mouth, and looked like an outlaw. Back out near the high cliffs I noticed that the young man was still on the rock.

"So long."

"Yep." He didn't look over his shoulder, just "Yep."

By night we were in Dubuque, Iowa. The sky was navy blue and the streets neon-lit and clean. They looked so safe I half

Pike's Point, McGregor, Iowa

expected to see one of those old-fashioned barbershop quartets leaning around a lamppost, singing. A theater marquee advertised HELEN REDDY / SATURDAY NIGHT / TWO SHOWS.

"You wanna see Helen Reddy?" I asked Stan. He rolled his eyes.

We checked into the Redstone Inn, a large Victorian-style building, "newly restored," said the clerk. Apples sat in a basket at the check-in counter. A sitting room to the left of the check-in desk was where they served high tea. Up the flight of stairs, there were baby chandeliers that shone. In our room thick quilts lay on the beds. Stan napped. I pulled stationery from a drawer and wrote a girl back in Boston, figuring since I wasn't too successful in wooing her up close, I might have better luck from afar. A breeze came in past the curtains and I tried to put some of the breeze in the letter.

"Stan?"

"Yeah, what?"

"Good night."

"Yeah, good night."

The lamplight from outside came in past the window, and some of the lamplight illuminated a corner of the letter, which leaned upright on the dresser lamp. I imagined the breeze and light might give the letter a magic I was unable to give it.

Next morning, before the sun had fully risen over the hills and glided along the rooftops and swept through the trees and down the alleys and streets of town, we were making our way to the local tackle shop to buy cane poles. The time had come to fish the river. We rode and found a little spot by the river, on the edge of town. A morning chill rested at our back. A man came off a nearby dock and I asked if this was a good fishing spot.

"Well, couple days ago some kids caught a mess of bass right around here."

I looked at Stan. "We're gonna catch some fish this morning."

Stan wouldn't touch the worms that squirmed in the white Styrofoam cup, so I baited both hooks. He swung his cane pole out over the river, but the wind blew the string right back at him. "Throw out sideways," I urged, and he did, and the string finally fell out across the river. After one hour, Stan said, "Something's wrong. I ain't even got a bite yet."

"Patience, buddy, patience."

A woman walked by, said, "Catch anything?" We both shook our head. Thirty minutes later we up and left. "We'll catch them when we get out on that river," I promised.

For dinner we went Italian: pepperoni pizza, extra cheese. I dropped two quarters into a table jukebox. Stan got the first choice and went for Sam Cooke's "You Send Me." I opted for

Dubuque, Iowa

Sinatra, "Summer Wind," 1965, Nelson Riddle conducting the orchestra. In 1965 the voice was there, between mellow and just perfect, old but a young old. Little candles burned atop the tables, which had red-checkered tablecloths. Men up at the bar yelled kindly at one another. Then the waitress began turning out the lights and it was time to go.

We strolled the main street, saw a man coming out of the local bank. It was nearing midnight.

"Looks strange," Stan said.

"Yeah, he could be messing with the money."

"Who knows?"

We turned a street and walked westward, to the river. A huge white boat sat anchored in the water. Down below the levee a dog barked at the waves as they came in and went out. Every now and then a wave would almost reach the dog, but it would jump back at the last moment. The dog would then resume its barking. Finally the dog left, walking downriver, its tail wagging, and disappeared in the darkness, its final set of barks muted, as if it were whispering. Then there was only the quiet whir of the river and its waves. The light on the river flickered like a candle laid on its side.

Davenport, Iowa

They played Class A professional baseball by the river in Davenport, Iowa, in the kind of stadium, if you like your old-fashioned baseball, you'd love: creaky wood bleachers, pigeons in the rafters, real grass on the field. We just walked through the stadium gate, up to the bleachers, and took seats, like scouts down from the big leagues looking for that unknown. It was early and there was no game going on. I leaned back on my seat, threw my legs up over the seat in front of me, and gave Stan a little Iowa baseball history:

On July 21, 1935, a scout for the Cleveland Indians, Cyril Slapnicka, stalked through the wheat fields in back of Bill Feller's farm over in Van Meter, Iowa. Neither Bill Feller nor his sixteen-year-old boy, Bob, heard Slapnicka turn his car engine off. It was as if he just rose up from the wheat.

"Howdy, I'm Cyril Slapnicka of the Cleveland Indians," he said. "That the boy they tell me is quite a pitcher?"

Bill Feller, looking at his boy, said yes, and the boy smiled.

Bob's dad used to string cord out back of the farmhouse, then hang lamps so the boy could practice his pitching at night.

Two days later Cy Slapnicka went to see young Bob pitch, watching the first few innings from under a tree on the outside of the ballpark, looking like a hick but knowing exactly

what he was after. For the last few innings he moved inside the stadium, and by game's end he knew the boy had magic in his arm. Bob Feller was signed up for the big leagues.

He was groomed in the minor leagues, then set the majors on fire. On April 16, 1940, which was opening day, he tossed a no-hit game against the Chicago White Sox. On April 30, 1946, he pitched another no-hit game, against the Yankees and their lovely hitter, Joe DiMaggio. In 1948 he led the league in strikeouts for the seventh straight year. He ended his career with a roomful of awards.

Down on the ballfield in Davenport, a groundskeeper laid out chalk in straight lines around the diamond.

"Shake hands with the man who shook hands with Babe Ruth," said William Montgomery, who had just come up on our blind side. The grin on his face was as wide as Iowa. He was seventy-three years old and tickled that two visitors had taken a shine to the stadium. There would be a game, he mentioned, in a few hours, and put his hand, visorlike, to his head, surveying the field. His eyes came to rest on another section of the bleachers, where workers were sweeping. "They're over from the mental hospital," he said.

Montgomery was president of the Quad Cities Baseball Association, the group that oversaw the stadium. "They were going to tear it down back in 1958 and put in *parking meters*," he said, his voice shrill. But in 1958, in Davenport, Iowa, the baseball fans railed and protested, and the stadium by the river stayed a stadium by the river.

Montgomery said, "Follow me," and started down the bleacher steps, pulling a handful of chained keys from his baggy pants, to open the door to his office. Beer bottles and popcorn boxes lay everywhere. He wanted to show us the pictures of the players who had come there to play, simple black-and-white pictures that lined the walls — young players with raw talent and older players who had to make do with fading talent.

Montgomery was itching to tell stories of some of the greats who had played there, like Satchell Page, the tall, brawny pitcher from the old Negro Leagues, a fifty-year-old man who passed this way on his way up to pitch for the Cleveland Indians. Page stood on the mound and kicked his leg high and threw the ball with dazzle, the ball smacking into the catcher's mitt before the dirt kicked up by his cleats had settled back to the ground.

Over in a corner sat a gravestone, smooth and gray, cool to the touch of a hand. The baseball association had just purchased it for their previous president. "We'll have a little ceremony and all, out on the field this summer," Montgomery said.

Davenport, Iowa

Twenty years ago the ballpark flooded, and waves from the Mississippi crashed into the stadium. "We picked catfish right out of the dugouts," he said, laughing at it still, pulling shut the door, making his way back up into the stadium bleachers. As he stepped into the sunlight from the shade of the underground part of the stadium, he said, "Y'all make sure to come back for the game this evening." And Stan, crazy for years about baseball, grinned like a kid.

We drove the town, then headed for the levee. A group of high schoolers were dressed in prom wear, walking and holding hands. The guys were in tuxedos and the girls wore pretty dresses — pink and yellow and green — that flapped in the wind coming off the river. As one guy kissed his girl, Stan snapped a picture, and the sun was falling over everything, as if to drape the scene with a serene *yes yes yes*. I thought of my high-school prom, which I didn't attend. Oh, there was a girl all right, but when I got around to asking her, she said no and said it with a smile, which hurt. On my prom night I shot basketball on warm cement in Columbus, Ohio, and dreamed of becoming a pro.

The guys and girls disappeared down the levee with the wind still plucking at the dresses of the young girls, who held them up, ladylike, about an inch from the ground, so they would not drag.

The fans in Davenport started coming a good hour before game time. The hometown team, the Quad Cities Angels, was to face the Peoria Chiefs. Quad Cities was holding down second place in the league, but Peoria was only two games behind. Little boys were walking around with baseball gloves on, pounding the center of their mitts with their fists. Girls were snickering, the tips of their fingers red from the cold soda in their hands. Grown men jawed about life and baseball. Peanut shells dropped between the cracks in the bleachers. Pigeons fluttered in the rafters. The waves in the river, just beyond centerfield, had started to kick up in the cool of evening. The game got under way.

By the end of the second inning the home team had a 2–1 lead, and by the end of the fifth, they had broken even further out front, 4–1. By the sixth inning the sun had begun to sink. Orange, it moved to the edge of the river as if pulled by a string. Dusk had served a blueness upon the river. It turned dark and the field was all lit up bright by big lights, and you could see mothers unfolding blankets to drape around their little girls; the little boys playing tough-guy roles, shunning the blankets.

In the seventh inning the Peoria team started to come back, 4–3, and we had a contest. A kid named Allan Peterson, for the home team, took a ball, then a strike, then swung his bat around with a vengeance, and you heard a moment's echo of the sweet

Davenport, Iowa

crack of the bat in the wind, which lifted the ball, which disappeared into the lights and sailed over the wall for a home run.

Then another hometown player, Dante Bichette, jerked one, and there was the same lone crack of the bat in the night wind, and the fans rose up beautifully, together, like a school of trout rising to the surface in the evening after moths. Bichette rounded third and trotted home, his gloved hand, his batting arm, appearing ominous and wonderful all at once.

The game ended 6–4, the local sportswriters had their story, and all the baseball players floated off the field and into the next day and game. Parents and their young ones strolled out the stadium gate. We could overhear the charming chatter of a "Wow!" here and a "Did you see that?" there, the words coming from the little ones, who seemed desperate to tell the world about the pigeons and bright lights and long-legged outfielders and home runs.

Some walked home. Some drove away. Before long the chatter was not there anymore and night had swallowed everyone.

During the late autumn of 1858, Abraham Lincoln and Stephen Douglas crisscrossed Illinois, playing before huge crowds and debating seven times on the great moral question of the day, slavery. There was a U.S. Senate seat at stake, and Lincoln had been wooed out of retirement by the Republican party; Douglas was the incumbent Democrat; Lincoln opposed the spread of slavery; Douglas promoted it. On October 13 of that year they squared off in Quincy, Illinois, and took to a podium set up in Washington Park.

Douglas was a short man, wide, with a wrestler's physique, and was referred to as "the little giant." He had a debater's voice, deep and direct as thunder. Lincoln was tall and thin and just shy of gaunt, his voice was said to be shrill. In the end the debates would be judged a draw, and the election won by Douglas. But Lincoln was the story, for in losing the election, he had somehow risen above it, the great moral question steering him on a course of purpose and destiny.

He was a lawyer, but not lawyerly. He knew much, but was wise enough to confess what he didn't know, confident enough he could learn. There was something mystical about him, but perhaps it was just his plainness. He was country, from the backwoods. Some did not see his brilliance at first, but days or weeks later, away from him, they would, just as they might see the fresh growth of a plant on coming back to it. And so at the age of forty-nine, he had been called forth, to warm a nation with the logic of moral certitude. Lincoln: there was even something hard and honest and American about the name. He was above a congressional seat. Illinois was dress rehearsal for the presidency. As president, his name would be scrawled beneath a document called the Emancipation Proclamation, and the slaves freed. His approach — logic over illogic, right over wrong, simplicity over complexity — would be so revered that other Republicans taking the same path would come to be known as "Lincoln Republicans."

Twilight was spreading like molasses as we walked through Washington Park, up to the spot where Lincoln had debated Douglas. There was a stone to mark the spot in the wide, green park. A wind whipped softly. A knot of teens were gathered nearby, yelling at passing cars. We headed for the Newcomb Hotel across the street.

A man named George, who was wearing the kind of cheap stretch Banlon shirt I wore in junior high school, was behind the counter of the cavernous hotel, which looked desolate. We startled George. "Hi," he said. "How ya doing? What time is it?"

I told him nine o'clock. He fumbled for room keys. He said he had been on the job less than six weeks. His marriage had gone bad. "Yep, I just woke up one day and my marriage was

over with. I just got out, just left. Hell, I'm not one for arguing and all that stuff."

Now and then, as George talked, a lone figure went up the hotel stairs, on tiptoes, in silence.

"I went home last week," he continued. "My daughter was having trouble. She got expelled from school. See, this guy came up from behind her and touched her and she turned around and chopped him. She's a third-degree black belt. He lost three front teeth."

We climbed two flights of steps, and found our rooms at the end of a dark hallway.

"Stan?"

"Yeah?"

"Put the chain on your door. This is a creepy place."

Come morning, we had the urge to go, to get, and did, skipping breakfast.

It took the better part of a day traveling down rural Missouri roads, but we found the tiny town of Florida, Missouri, which wasn't on the Rand McNally map. Ten people lived there, though someone said it could be as many as twelve.

It was here, on November 30, 1835, that Samuel Clemens — later Mark Twain — was born. Now it was pretty much a forgotten town, a one-road town. There were two houses on the left side of the road, three houses on the right side, a trailer and an abandoned house down the road, and no place in town to get a cup of hot coffee. A bronze marker near the crossroads indicated the spot of land where Clemens was born.

We knocked on several doors, and getting no answer, followed the path that led to the trailer. A man came out the door and peered at us through the vines that hung from the awning of the trailer. Floyd Rouse, fifty-five, turned out to be a disabled truck driver who lived there with his mother.

"Yep, it's just us and the Yates family lives here now. The Yateses moved down here from Hannibal," Floyd said, turning his head away, as if to wonder why the Yateses would do such a thing. He pulled a little comb from his back pocket and laid it to his head all in one motion, sweeping his hair back.

Asked why he continued to live there, Floyd said, putting the comb back in his pocket, "Well, we been trying to sell for a couple years."

His mother, Alice, stood nearby, her hands in the pockets of her robe, her hair done up in curlers. "There used to be a bank, a clothing store, a drugstore," she said.

When she paused, the son picked right up, "And a barbershop, a hotel, and a doctor's office."

Quincy, Illinois

"And don't forget," the mother finished, "we had a blacksmith shop too." Everything was gone from Florida, and before the hour was out, we were too.

When he was an infant, Twain's parents brought the family forty-five miles down the road, to Hannibal, where he would spend his childhood. Mark Twain made his last visit to Hannibal in 1902, when he was sixty-seven. He was feted and trailed by crowds. Reporters hustled for quotes. Women gawked.

A dinner was thrown on Twain's behalf by John and Louise Cruikshank, who lived in Rockcliff, a mansion perched on a hill and looking toward the river. John and Louise had three daughters and they all were at the dinner honoring Twain. One of the daughters, Helen, now ninety-three, was ten when she met Mark Twain.

She sat in an armchair in her lovely home, surrounded by the kind of quiet style and elegance encouraged by old money. Green-and-white wicker furniture sat on the front porch, antique furniture in the living and dining rooms. Fresh flowers filled a vase to the left of the piano. Across the kelly-green lawn, Rockcliff, her parents' mansion, still stood.

"There were maids all over the place," she said, referring to the Twain visit. "My sisters and I were the only children allowed. It was going to be a special event. The people were walking up the hill to our place. Some came in horses and buggies. Of course there were no automobiles. Mark Twain himself came in a carriage. I noticed when he got out of the carriage he stopped and talked to all the people." The memory brought a smile as delicate as the lace curtains that hung from the windows.

"I remember how proud I was when my father took me over and introduced me to Mr. Twain, who said to me, 'Which one of the daughters are you?' He seemed very tall. He had a big gold chain and watch around his waist. I remember his white hair. His voice was slow. After he made his talk, most of the guests left. A few of his friends went to the dining room. I went through the dining room to the pantry. I could see what was going on. A lady named Mrs. Garth was trying to use one of those long ear trumpets and Twain couldn't understand and everyone was laughing."

A large wooden desk sat at Helen's right elbow, a desk her father carved out of a piano, especially for her. She wore a light shade of pink fingernail polish, a gray outfit, flat-heeled shoes. Having lived all her life in Hannibal, she could recall days when she would take a skiff across the Mississippi River to go shopping and dancing with girlfriends. "The levee is not as attractive as it once was," she said.

She once trained here in Hannibal to be a concert singer, but never pursued singing as a career.

Helen Knighton, Hannibal, Missouri

There was a love of her life. "I married a Hannibal man," said Helen Cruikshank Knighton. The comment had come out with a gust of affection, and it made one wonder: were there any men on earth worth marrying other than Hannibal men? There were never any children and now there was no husband. When she had time to worry she worried about the flowers in the garden. "The peonies are starting to bloom," she said, and April had blossomed into May.

Samuel Clemens had been a printer, a miner, a riverboat pilot, a vagabond journalist, and a Bohemian before it was fashionable to be one. He walked into rooms to yank the curtains back farther, to throw light on what he couldn't quite make out.

He came riding out of the West — the "Wild Humorist of the Pacific" — in 1864 and would make his reputation along the East Coast as a writer, humorist, and lecturer. He arrived in time for the Civil War and hitched up with the Confederacy, but left after two weeks: the bullets were real and war no place for a humorist.

He loved his country, and yet became famous for lampooning it. He called Congress a "distinctively native criminal class." He was called a "vulgar comic," among other things, and welcomed controversy like a cup of warm tea. He posed for pictures, hands on hips, chin out, as if he were a potentate.

He courted the lovely Olivia Langdon of Elmira, New York, an heiress with an impressive family background. When he asked her to marry him she said no, and there was popular opinion that her family thought him wild, unpredictable, loud. But a man who is truly in love will come back from a no the way the sun comes back after a storm, and will say everything again, more softly. So he asked again and they married in 1870 in Hartford, Connecticut. They would keep moving over the years, the vagabond in him never tamed.

He referred to himself as a "scribbler of books and an immovable fixture among the other rocks of New England." He had changed his name to Mark Twain; *mark twain* actually being a river term meaning two fathoms deep.

Guns and bloodshed and evil-eyed men were no strangers to him, but figures and scenes from his childhood.

He was not teahouse-smooth, but was said to be well mannered. He had a kind of grace that was rugged, true, like something fashioned from rock. He was always handsome, but grew more handsome when he stepped beyond middle age, because

Mark Twain's house, Hannibal, Missouri

then his face seemed captured in its own light and was protected by its own shadows.

He did most of his writing in a study that overlooked the blue hills of Elmira, New York, where he summered with his wife and her family.

Gin was his preferred drink. Pool — eight ball in the corner pocket — his favorite sport. Beethoven was his favorite composer, though he was known to tap out old negro spirituals on the piano in the evenings, recalling his childhood, delighting his wife. He smoked a corncob pipe, wore white suits, loved children, adored cats.

Mark Twain went into the newspaper business in Buffalo, New York. He constantly argued with readers, questioning their intellect. He recoiled at the necessity to operate a newspaper like a business and finally just quit, slamming the door behind him.

He lived in a time of great inventions, and he saw barons throw money into land where towns sprouted and railroads spread.

He grew despondent with America during the 1870s, saw greed climbing fast up over hills and said it would ruin the country. His heart still beat passionately, but his causes were not the same: Civil War blood had stained his river, railways killed his steamboat era. The clock was moving too fast.

In 1882 Mark Twain journeyed the Mississippi River once again, to do research for his book *Life on the Mississippi.* As much as he was delighted to see things and places he had known when he was young, when the river was in his front pocket, he was also saddened, the way an older man might be saddened when he goes to look for a certain woman he had known in his youth. He hopes for a little glimmer of the woman he once knew, but he sees only the vase; the flowers have disappeared.

As he was approaching his fiftieth year, Mark Twain began thinking of a book about a boy and a slave, against the backdrop of a river. *The Adventures of Huckleberry Finn* is the book that has come to define the man. It was published to modest acclaim, but now it seems permanently located in the literary consciousness of the world.

The book is as simple as it is sophisticated. There is Huck, a rebel, a boy who is a little bit of every boy, and there is Jim, his friend, a black slave running from the chains. And there is that river.

One of the most poignant scenes in literature takes place when Huck argues with his conscience about whether or not to turn Jim in. He holds the letter in his hand that he has written to Miss Watson, the letter that will betray Jim. "I was a trembling, because I'd got to decide forever betwixt two things, and I

Tom and Huck, Hannibal, Missouri

knowed it. I studied for a minute, sort of holding my breath, and then says to myself, 'All right, then, I'll *go* to hell,' and tore it up."

Mark Twain has been called a racist because of his use of the word *nigger* in *Huckleberry Finn*. It is a very serious thing to call a man a racist, and it is a tricky endeavor to go into the shadows of a man's mind.

Consider these facts: after a lynching occurred in his home state of Missouri, Mark Twain wrote an essay, "The United States of Lyncherdom," that is as direct an attack against lynching as has ever been written in America.

In 1885 he wrote a letter to the Yale Law School explaining that he wanted to help pay the tuition of a black law school student. There is a sadness, a brutal eloquence to the tenor of the letter. "I do not believe I would cheerfully help a white student who would ask a benevolence of a stranger, but I do not feel so about the other color. We have ground the manhood out of them, & the shame is ours, not theirs; & we should pay for it."

Mark Twain simply doted on his wife, wrote love letters to her throughout their marriage. "I love you, my darling, and this my love will increase step by step as tooth by tooth falls out, milestoning my way down to this great mystery and sweet bye and bye."

He had four children and saw three of them die from illness, leaving him with the kind of hurt that would leave his body only when his heart stopped beating.

In the 1870s he began making poor investments, particularly in a typesetting machine, and by 1895 was broke. The hand of an aging man was forced and he had no cards to lay on the table, so he packed and went on the lecture circuit again, bumping across the country and around the world by train and boat, his wife at his side, his creditors watching his every move.

He was no longer so witty as he had been, but he had reached a point of fame where he could simply step onto a stage and there would be laughter, and that laughter would propel him on to the next town and the next stage.

All the while he was growing bitter about the "damned human race." But there would be personal redemption as he worked himself out of debt. The crowds thought it a marvelous comeback, the newspapers played up the story, and once again he was tipping his hat, winking, letting the old wit fly.

He called river people "my own class" of people, and late in life, when sentiments had begun to creep, he referred to himself as the human race's "oldest friend."

His wife, Olivia, a frail woman, was often ill and bedridden. He sought cures, turned toward mysticism, gnawed at the edges

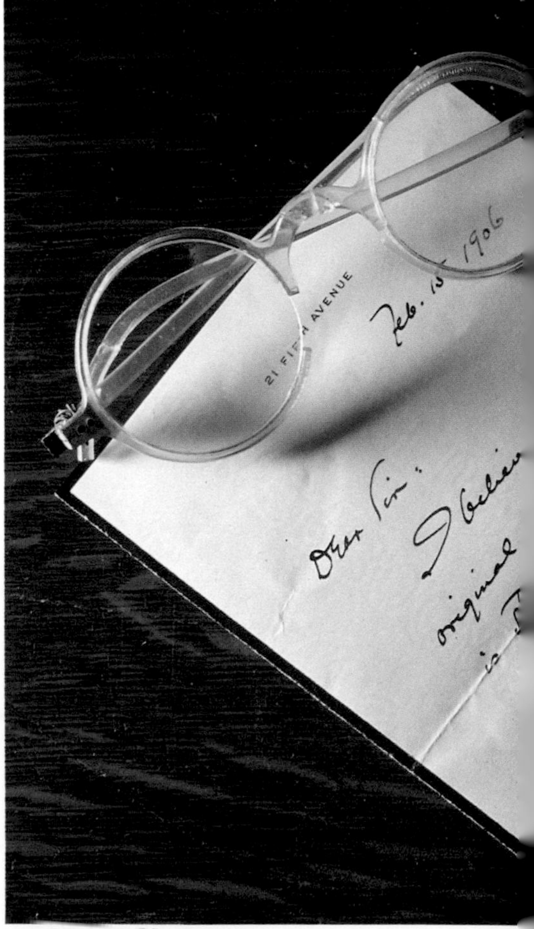

Letter from Mark Twain

of science, anything to keep her. In October of 1893 they went to Florence, Italy, and that is where she died, of heart failure. For the first time in a long time there was no pretty woman to kiss in the evening, to read poetry to. His spirit grew weak as a daisy in a storm.

Broken, he moved to New York City, strolled Fifth Avenue as though he owned it, became a museum piece, a legend on the windowsill of a nation. Bored, he bolted from New York City as impulsively as he had arrived, and took off for another around-the-world journey, laughing to keep from crying.

He never graduated from high school, yet there he was in 1907 at Oxford, receiving an honorary degree, posing on the lawn after the ceremony with his chest stuck out, as if to damn the whole affair.

Perhaps the most telling picture of Twain was taken when he was seventy. He was leaning on a bed in the picture, his face half lit, his eyes moist. He did not look old, just sad and sweet and lonely. The white hair was all over the place, charging the world. That quiet strong gaze seemed directed at something only he could see, perhaps that white suit in the corner. It would have been nice to hustle down to the river one more time.

"The twentieth century is not my century," Mark Twain said, and he died April 21, 1910, after slipping into a coma at his home in Redding, Connecticut. Those at his bedside said there was hardly a sound. It was as if he simply drifted out the window, up into the clouds, that white suit on his back. Halley's Comet had been in the sky at his birth and at his death, and many attached mystical significance to the coincidence.

The funeral was in New York City. Thousands came. William Dean Howells, the man who published Twain in *The Atlantic Monthly,* was there. "I looked a moment at the face I knew so well; and it was patient with the patience I had so often seen in it; something of a puzzle, a great silent dignity, an assent to what must be from the depths of a nature whose tragical seriousness broke in the laughter which the unwise took for the whole of him."

One imagines Mark Twain to lie somewhere near this river, so that the sand and mud and warmth and cold and morning-prettiness of the river could all move past his stone. But he wanted to lie with his family, next to Olivia and the children in the Woodlawn Cemetery in Elmira, New York. His stone says SAMUEL LANGHORNE CLEMENS — MARK TWAIN — NOVEMBER 30, 1835–APRIL 21, 1910. It was a double existence, and full of thunder.

The world is left with the books that tell the man's life, where he went and how he got there.

Hannibal, Missouri

As we approached the Hannibal harbor we spotted Bart Bussink, our raft builder. His back was to us, and his shoulders bent to the raft as he hammered nails. Before we reached Bart, I kept looking at the raft and the river, treating them visually as one. The raft looked small and the river big.

Bart spotted us, then let his face break into a slow grin. "Well, what do you think?" he asked.

"Looks nice," Stan said.

"Great," I followed.

A man sitting in a boat said, "So you two are the ones going downriver on *that* thing." Fred Shelton's legs were crossed, his hands resting on his knees, the laid-back harbormaster.

"They don't pay me enough to get excited about this job," Shelton said. "And anyway, I'm gonna eat three meals a day whether I come to work or not." Fred Shelton had survived two heart attacks. He was calling the shots now, sitting by the river as the days rolled by.

When Bart arrived in Hannibal he had no luck finding a secure place to build the raft. Someone told him to call Fred Shelton. Bart looked the number up in the phone book. Fred said, "No problem. Come on down to the harbor in the morning."

Bart was twenty-seven and was born in Amsterdam, Holland. He was always good at doing things with his hands, a tinkerer, a Mr. Fixit from way back. Where others saw only scraps of wood, Bart saw birdhouses, doghouses, cabins. By the time he was in high school he was nearly professional. Something would break down at home and he'd watch everyone go to pieces trying to fix it, then he'd step in, mend whatever it was that was broken, and lope away. Didn't date much in high school; always out building something.

Bart went to Hampshire College in Amherst, Massachusetts. After college he moved to Boston and built his own loft. He talked his dad into helping him buy a building company. The business lasted only about a year. Bart found business too restricting for his gentle, Bohemian soul; unfinished paperwork did him in.

Stan met Bart at dinner one night back in Boston and, hearing that he was a builder, asked him if he could build a raft. "Sure, no problem," Bart said, and overnight threw together a cardboard replica.

When Bart showed up in Hannibal he had no fancy-drawn plans of the raft, just a suitcase with two hundred pounds of tools and a backpack with some clothing. He'd build the raft from his mind, from sheer know-how. He hired a local guy and paid him four dollars an hour. Then, two days into the job, he had to fire him: drinking on the job. Bart meant business. The next day he hired another guy, who worked out fine.

One night, halfway through building the raft, Bart woke up in his motel room, flicked on the lights. He was worrying that the raft wasn't right, that it was sitting too low, was too heavy, that the flotation would not be right. He hustled down to the harbor at dawn and started taking the raft apart, starting all over. The man whom he had hired thought Bart had flipped, but Bart told him there was no time for questions.

By evening, Bart was putting the finishing touches on the raft. I pulled out a 5 x 7 glossy of Mark Twain and placed it on the raft. Bart smiled.

Hannibal was hosting a six-month celebration in honor of Mark Twain's sesquicentennial. Some in the city said the event was too long, that city officials had gone hard for celebrity worship at the expense of common city services.

“They’re down there fooling with all those Mark Twain houses and I can’t even get a light on my street fixed,” complained Katherine Latta. She was referring to the white homes, trimmed in green, on Hill Street where Mark Twain grew up and where his father practiced law. It was the section of Hannibal that drew the tourists, who could be seen walking around in the early morning, quietly, as if walking through a museum.

The city did lean hard on Twain’s name. A fast-food shop, a few stores, a motel, a hotel — all bore some semblance of his name or the characters he created. I walked into the tourist bureau and asked the woman behind the desk if she thought it all a little much. With her forefinger, she pushed her glasses up off her nose.

“Too much? You ever go to Springfield? Springfield, Illinois? You ought to see what they do to Lincoln’s name over there.” Her voice had grown edgy and she stared me out the door.

On a street, later in the day, a woman with a kind face stopped us and asked, “Are you the two fellas traveling the river?” Word had spread.

“Yes,” we said, our voices one.

She took a step closer, her purse swinging on her wrist. “Tell me, did you start up there at the headwaters?”

“Yes.”

“Is it true that you can walk across the river up there, just walk right across it?”

When Stan said, “Yep,” she lifted her hand to her lips. “Oh my.”

It is still possible to stand on the corner of Hill Street in Hannibal, on the steps of the house that Mark Twain lived in, and look to your left, where the Mississippi River flows, and understand how it pulled a young boy downriver. Clouds open. Steamboats pass. A moon rises. You cannot look at the river, when you are on a street and level with it, and not want to step down to the edge, to ponder it.

On a late summerlike evening, the air calm, as sweet as something young and light, John Fogle stood down at the levee. He was a nineteen-year-old shell diver who started diving right after high school, who never so much as looked at a college application. He always knew he’d dive for shells. His granddaddy, he said, used to dive for shells, and he had sat at his knee and listened to the stories.

His hands were stuffed into the pockets of his jeans. He longed to explain the lure of diving. “It’s just the feeling of being out there. It’s the old mighty Mississippi. I don’t know what it’d be like to be away from the river.” He would be at home in the evenings and sometimes just break for the front door, “to come down here just to look at the current,” he said.

Catfish

There was the slightest bit of red hair on his round face. His eyes were quick with blinks. "I found a pearl in a shell once. Big as the button on your shirt. It was so clear you could almost see yourself in it."

A light splash was heard in the water. "Catfish. They start jumping in the evening." He got the words out before the rings caused by the splash had a chance to fade into the calmness of the river.

There was a riverboat out on the water, brightly lit, all dressed up and headed downriver.

Darkness began to drop. The young shell diver walked away, toward home, across railroad tracks and grass climbing up to his knees. When he got about twenty yards he turned and yelled, "Hey, look at the river. Ain't she beautiful?"

The next morning we bought a few more supplies for the raft journey to New Orleans. And in the evening we took Harbormaster Fred Shelton and his wife, Suzie, along with Bart, out to dinner, to a little restaurant a stone's throw up off the river.

Fred and Suzie were living on the outskirts of Hannibal. "At night out there we don't hear nothing but animals," he said. They had a little pond in the backyard. Suzie would come down to the river with a fishing pole on some evenings to fish. What she caught she would take home and toss in the backyard pond.

The chatter was high and light with everyone talking about the raft journey: Would we actually do it? Would we ever be heard from again? There was a toast: "To Huck and Jim."

Forty minutes passed, then fifteen more, and still no steaks and ribs. Fred complained to the waitress and she explained that the regular cook had been thrown in jail the night before — drunk driving — and the new cook, just hired, was having a hell of a time in the kitchen. When the meal finally arrived, Fred's appetite seemed ruined. Later, as we prepared to leave the restaurant, Fred cut a path over to the waitress.

"Now, I'm harbormaster in this town. I don't know if you know that or not. But I'm probably one of the last people you want to make wait all day for a meal. Don't you know that the people getting off the boats down there at the harbor ask me for places they can go and eat? I can tell you this: I won't be sending none of them up here."

Fred's wife inched her way over to him and tugged on his elbow. Fred turned, put a cigarette to his lips, and walked out of the restaurant in long, slow strides, a gunslinger's walk.

Everyone stood outside in the parking lot, enveloped in the darkness. The river looked smooth as a cat's back. Fred looked down at the river, then at us. "I still can't believe you're going on that raft." He smiled, said good-bye, and he and his wife walked away, holding hands. We bade farewell to Bart. "You guys'll be okay," he said reassuringly. Bart would be flying back to Boston. We walked down to the raft to sleep the night.

When we got to the raft we noticed two men sitting in the dark on the side of a building about sixty yards away. A light bulb on the side of the building threw their shadows against the building, and for a moment it looked as though four men were watching us. We eyed them hard and let our imaginations race, figuring they were planning to jump us after we fell asleep.

"They'll get a surprise," Stan said, and I said, "They sure will," even if I didn't quite know what the surprise would be.

We checked the raft for sturdiness and wondered aloud if we were ready. Bugs circled the light bulb at the top of the harbor light post. The raft rocked gently from the lapping of the waves. We heard footsteps in the dark. The first thing to come into view was a dark shadow, then the tip of a lit cigarette that burned orange. The harbor light caught the face: it was Fred Shelton again. He got so close that we could see his tongue in his mouth. He took a drag off the cigarette.

"You know, I've made many mistakes in my life." Stan glanced up at me without turning his head. "Some of the mistakes have been costly. And I didn't learn from them until it was too late." He flicked the ash tip from his cigarette and the ashes drifted down toward his feet. The wind picked them up and carried them out to the surface of the river, where they died.

"Don't go out on that river if you don't know what you're doing. It'll kill you." He glanced at the river, then back at us. His speech finished, he said good-bye, turned and walked away in that slow gunslinger walk of his, and disappeared through the dark. The last thing we heard was his car tires rolling over gravel,

I repeated Fred's words — "It'll kill you" — and they hung in the air like sad violin music.

"We didn't need to hear no midnight death talk," Stan said.

"Hell no," I said.

And suddenly, the dark we were standing in seemed darker. I strained my eyes across the river and couldn't see the other side. We unrolled the sleeping bags.

A couple of hours later there was a loud bang on the side of the raft, as though someone had slapped it. We bolted up. Stan reached for the flashlight, I groped for the pocketknife, and there we were, pacing the dock, seeing no one, shaken.

"Maybe it was just a wave," I said, noticing that the two men who had been at the side of the building sixty yards away were now gone. It was 3:30. We tried sleeping more but couldn't, so we rose at 4:30, in the dark, dew still on the leaves of the nearby trees, stars still in the sky. Things seemed dreamy.

Jackson Island, Missouri

We brushed our teeth in the morning chill and decided it was time to go. We loosened the rope that held the raft to the harbor and drifted away through the mist. Stan stood at the front of the raft, one leg bent, an explorer. The all-night lights of Hannibal got smaller as we got farther out, and then the harbor itself disappeared behind the mist. The river seemed to rise and spread all at once. The raft followed the current, and pretty soon, morning light came down from the sky.

On a raft out in the middle of the Mississippi River the land seemed to come at us as we floated, and then the land seemed to pass right through our bodies. The raft was small and the river big and those are the facts that would always be on the mind. Homes leaned on bluffs. Land sloped in small arcs. Silence fed silence.

Four miles downriver we rafted over to Jackson Island, our first stop. Stan jumped from the raft onto the island and tied the rope around a tree. I clapped my hands. We walked the floor of the island, soft and muddy, passing tree trunks nibbled at by chipmunks, listening to the island come alive with the sounds of birds that screeched at our presence as we traveled deeper into the greenness of the island. Upon meeting the river on the other side, we turned and walked back to the raft and rafted into the distance. The morning light had brightened even more.

I spoke of Fred Shelton and his visit the night before. It may have been awkward and his words a bit ungraceful, but he meant well, right?

"Yeah, he meant well," Stan said.

We rafted into evening, and that moment between evening and dark, when things seemed shadowy and eternal, passed into night. We drifted toward the west bank of the river, looking for a spot to anchor. A little boy was crouched and fishing from the bank.

"Hey, do you know what town we're near?"

"What?" he said, now standing, his eyes glued to the raft.

"Do you know what town we're near?"

"Hamburg," he yelled.

We drifted closer, agreeing it was as good a place as any to anchor, and the boy suddenly grabbed his fishing pole and bucket and bolted up the hill into the woods. The tail of his sweatshirt flew straight out behind him, flat as a pancake. Strangers on a raft. No wonder.

We tied the raft to a tree that leaned over a bank of huge rocks and began to think of dinner. There was no food! We had done all kinds of last-minute chores in Hannibal but had forgotten to shop for food. A crisis. Through the trees above the bank there was the glimmer of lights. Stan said he would try to bum a ride and make it into town. "Good idea," I told him.

He climbed the rocks and went up and over a fence. I watched his back, a dog barked in the distance, and he was gone.

I looked around, wanting to fix my eyes on things familiar, but everything was strange. So I rocked with the raft, hummed, stared at the sky, mostly black, though there were sprinkles of white, like talcum powder, breaking up the black. And there was the moon, moving slowly, doing its thing.

An hour passed. It seemed like two. Then I heard Stan's voice cry out, "We got food!" I jumped from the raft and directed the flashlight so he could step with the line of light and not break his neck coming across the jagged rocks. His face was red with happiness as he explained that he had knocked on a door, and before he had been able to finish his sad tale of two guys on the river

with no food, a woman and her daughter were tossing food into a brown paper bag.

He emptied the contents of the bag hurriedly; there was an assortment of foods. We fried frankfurters and beans in a skillet and ate beside the warm glow that burned from the Coleman lantern. There was bread to tear in half and to sop up the bean juice, milk to wash it all down, a woman and her daughter to say a prayer for.

Waves rocked the raft all night. Soon they became a natural part of our hearing and no longer seemed an intrusive sound, but a melody of the mind. The chill was steady and the brushing of trees sounded like the *rush rush* of barefooted children climbing steps.

Sleep on a raft on a river under the sky and you feel the first light of morning before it has gotten into the corners of your eyes, and when full morning arrives you are already up and heading downriver.

Drifting away, slow, silently, from the world it seemed, growing drowsy with the day, nothing but the iced-tea brown river and the land and the sky. Butterflies appeared out of nowhere. Birds circled the raft, as if to welcome, then fluttered away on wings light as lace. Fish jumped. Ripples swirled. The raft took the bends gracefully. And sometimes there were spots of water where there was no current, no ripples, just dead water, mystery.

Ten miles from Hamburg the raft slowed, began to drag, then came to a shocking stop, in the middle of the river. We grabbed oars and measured and were not at all amused that we had let ourselves drift out of the channel and onto a sandbar. Barges big as gray elephants passed, and we realized our danger. We would have to get in the water and push the raft back out into deeper water. Just as we began to take our shoes off, a fisherman in a boat came near.

"I'll tell you this: you get in that water with your shoes off and those shells will cut your feet all to pieces." He had on reflector glasses and as the sun bounced off them, it seemed that the glasses were doing the talking.

We put our shoes back on and stepped slowly into the river and grunted and pushed the raft off the sandbar back into deeper water. The shells felt sharp. After we were out in the channel we climbed back onto the raft. I turned in a burst of excitement to thank the fisherman. He was gone, but my eyes caught up with him downriver, drifting under shade.

At noon we anchored the raft near a bridge and behind some green bushes, concealing it as much as possible from potential thieves, then walked across the bridge past the WELCOME TO CLARKSVILLE, MISSOURI, sign.

The buildings of the old river town — brown, rust, gray — blended into one another. Old men in straw hats walked slowly. Women shopped. No children were in sight. A taxi driver sat behind the wheel. Slow day.

At the edge of the little commercial district, two men stood in a yard, one doing yard work and the other talking to the one doing yard work. Greetings. Randolph Brown arose from the stoop, took off a glove, switched the grass cutter to the still-gloved hand. He shook my hand, then Stan's, then introduced the other man as his brother, Willie Brown.

"It's just a little dying town," Randolph Brown said. The voice was a soft monotone. Most of his life, he said, he'd been a handyman right here in town. His brother used to do the same kind of work, but not now.

"I'm seventy-two years old now," Willie Brown said. "A man seventy-two ain't got no business working."

Randolph, who was seventy-three, said, "I been out there on that river once. I said, 'Lord, if you get me off this river this time, I'll never get myself out here again.'" He got off and never went back. "I say let the river be. Just let the river be."

In a fish and bait store we bought worms to fish with, then walked back down the main street of town. The laughter of women drew us into a used-furniture shop. It was dimly lit, which gave the women, who were sitting down, the advantage of making out our faces before we could make out theirs as we crossed into their store from the sunlight.

"Y'all ain't from Clarksville," one woman hollered right out.

"Nope. Boston," I said. Then Stan said, "Traveling the river."

We were encouraged to look at pictures of sons and daughters and nieces and nephews that hung on the wall. One woman looked at me, then pointed to a picture on the wall, her niece, and said, "You married?" Folks laughed.

The furniture sagged. Stan spotted a yellow cushion. He plopped onto it. It was dirty but soft. The softness appealed to him. "This'll be good for sitting on the raft."

"Two dollars," a woman said. Stan pulled two dollar bills out of his pocket and unballed them and flattened them for the woman. As we walked out the door there was more laughter, the same that originally drew us inside.

We purchased a few things, things that wouldn't perish. "Don't worry about dinner tonight," I said to Stan. "We'll be eating fish for dinner."

The taxi driver got our business, took us back to the bridge. Just as he crossed it, I told him to stop. Confused, he looked through the rearview mirror. "Where y'all headed?"

"Downriver. New Orleans."

"How you traveling?"
"Raft."
"Raft?" He turned all the way around in his seat.
An afternoon's fishing from the raft yielded nothing.
"Something's wrong," Stan said, wondering if we would have fish for dinner. We changed tactics. We took bread and wetted it and stuck little pieces of it onto the end of the hooks. We still caught no fish, so we anchored and dined on peanut butter and jelly sandwiches, drank orange juice, bit apples down to their core. No one mentioned fish again. Dark came innocently and sank into the river. The Coleman lantern gave light. Stan tinkered with his cameras. I wrote. The raft rocked us to sleep and, just before dawn, rocked us from sleep.

An unlit neon sign leaning over the bank ten miles downriver told us where we would have breakfast. As we angled the raft toward the bank, a man came out of the yellow house and crossed his lawn, heading in our direction. A dog followed him, barking. Then a woman came out of the house, stopped on the lawn, hands on her waist, and stared out onto the river at us. The man said hello and we said hello and in the same breath I asked if we could buy something to eat there.

"Yep, you can get something to eat," he said.

The woman was his wife, and she had come close enough to hear the talk about eating. "I got cheeseburgers and barbecue," she said.

"That'll do just fine."

In her Batchtown, Illinois, kitchen, Delores Hodgkinson pulled out a frying pan and grabbed some burgers from the freezer. Jim, her husband, took a seat at the table. It was just a makeshift restaurant out back of their house, with a few tables and chairs and a minikitchen.

Jim and Delores used to live over in East St. Louis. They were in building and decorating: he'd build a home, she'd decorate it, they'd move in, then someone would offer them a nice piece of dough and they'd sell. They did this over and over — the Jim and Delores show.

"I was young then," she said, and Jim, his neck craned over a cup of coffee, laughed.

The fire for city living began to flicker out for them a few years back. They came over from East St. Louis one day and spotted this little nick of land by the river.

"We got to have it," the husband said, and the wife said, "I know."

They figured they'd throw up a little diner, cater to river people, live off savings if need be, stare out at the river in the evenings, what the hell, relax.

"Never thought I'd be the one turning burgers and slinging hash," Delores said.

They loved it and made enough to get by. Nobody out here was trying to get rich or make the *Wall Street Journal.* Heck, Jim Hodgkinson just put the neon sign up that year, three years since they'd bought the place.

Jim woke up one morning and saw an elderly man standing on the lawn with a bowie knife in his hand and engaged in a standoff with the dog. The man had come up off the river in the middle of the night and pitched a tent: squatter's rights. Jim ran toward the man.

"What the hell are you doing?" he said. "Put that knife away."

The man wheeled toward Jim and said, "That dog's gonna attack me."

"No he ain't," Jim said, still pleading. "Put that knife away."

The man finally did. Then, with barely a word, not offering where he came from or where he was headed, he folded up his tent, got in his boat, and left.

There was the time a lone woman came by in a canoe. "She came in here and ordered a six-pack and drank every one of 'em before our eyes," said Delores.

"Whew," said Jim, shaking his head, remembering.

The woman paid the bill and walked out the door to her canoe. Jim and Delores sat in the kitchen. Jim parted the curtains and watched her through the window. Then he got up and walked quickly down to the canoe.

"Ain't you afraid to be traveling the river alone?" he asked.

The woman looked at Jim Hodgkinson. She reached under a piece of cloth in a corner of the canoe, pulled out a .38-caliber pistol, waved it at him, and sped away.

After our cheeseburger breakfast, Delores Hodgkinson took the leftovers and threw them out the door. The dog gobbled them up. Jim stood on the bank and waved as we rafted away. The dog stood by his knee, barking.

Back on the river, drifting, breathing with the flow of things, we ignored direction and moved around a bend and through a grove of trees that had spread across the river. We drifted off the main channel. It seemed like three rivers were around us. A man back in Hannibal had said that if we ever got lost, to throw a piece of paper onto the river and it would automatically flow in the direction of the current and the main channel of the river.

I tore a small piece of paper from a bag, tossed it in the river, and it headed back out to the main channel, showing the way.

St. Louis, Missouri

Night came and the air was edged by noise, a kind of distant and soft noise, tingly, that you might get from wind chimes.

Morning, rafting. Towns rose on the banks. Church bells rang out. It must have been Sunday. Trains roared by along the riverbank. Families sat on the land, fishing, picnicking.

In the evening we crossed the Mississippi where the Missouri River pours into it and had to use the emergency motor on the back of the raft because the current was swift and fast as the two rivers met. We made it across and then into the ten-mile-long channel that would take us into St. Louis.

After two hours in the channel we spotted the lights of St. Louis at the right-hand edge of the river. They were bright and soft and seemed to beckon. It was eleven o'clock as we reached the city. The sky was all blue and red and orange, and there was a dash of pink there too. St. Louis rose before our eyes with the bright lights reflecting in the water and the St. Louis arch sweeping over everything. Lights spilled from the levee, and a jazz combo went at it inside one of the anchored dining boats as couples strolled around chatting. Because we couldn't hear the music, it all looked like a silent movie. A jackbooted policeman stood tall up on the levee, arms folded across his chest.

We looked for a place to anchor, paddling around in circles on the raft. I turned my head away from land to the river that was at our back and screamed at Stan because a barge was about to engulf us. I screamed louder, "Turn the raft! Turn the raft!" We fumbled for oars, now both of us screaming, the barge still coming, and managed to elude the barge, but caught its heavy wake and rocked hysterically.

The lights of the city had suddenly lost their romance. The jackbooted policeman had watched it all, still as a mummy.

Finally we spotted a railing alongside an opening where a steamboat was anchored. We tied up the raft and sat on the railing to catch our breath and to watch the waves that were still jumping from the barge's wake. We looked up at the steamboat, and it said *Huck Finn*.

A small knot of people had gathered on the levee to gawk at us, but we vanished up the hill right before their eyes.

Aimless walking the next morning carried us right to the door of the Sunshine Mission. Before I could say anything, the man in the doorway said, "Round the back and through the alley." It sounded like an order, so we went around the back and through the alley. Men were gathered in back of the church. They were homeless and had come for sustenance, a meal, prayer. We stepped through the door. A man said, "Welcome, Brothers."

A man in shirtsleeves was screaming from the pulpit. "If God hadn't of saved you, you'd of been in hell by now."

St. Louis, Missouri

The audience numbered about forty, all men. Some had a grocery bag full of clothes, some had a cot rolled up and tied with string. Some listened in rapt attention. Others dozed off, their heads going from side to side as if barely connected to their necks.

Bibles lay on laps, open to indiscriminately turned-to pages. A poster on a wall asked HOW LONG HAS IT BEEN SINCE YOU WROTE HOME?

Following the sermon, everyone filed upstairs for the meal. Each man took a seat at a long table. The chairs were those hard folding chairs you see in high-school cafeterias. Lima beans and white bread and a cookie were served to each man. The lima beans were overcooked. The cookie was too hard. The bread was just fine.

A big man in navy whites stood at the doorway of the kitchen where the food had been prepared. Several men complained about the food, and the man in navy whites removed their plates and showed them to the door. "Go on now," he said. Several cursed at him in low tones. He paid no attention.

I stood and said, "We're traveling the river and if there's anyone in here who can tell us what to expect downriver, well, we'd appreciate any information."

There was silence. Then a man raised his head and said, "Stay off the river."

"What?"

"Stay off the river."

"Why?"

"Dangerous. The river's dangerous."

Another man from the back yelled out, "Only thing I can tell you about the river is when you get in trouble call the Coast Guard." That drew laughter.

Following the meal, some of the men gathered in the back alley. Many said they were not headed to any special place, just taking in the land. Some stood around, fidgeting like newly enlisted recruits. Some walked quickly away, as if they had appointments to keep. A man named Earl Clay came up and bummed coffee money from us.

A block away, we stood at the back of a parking lot where another group of men was gathered. They sat on crates under a big tree, playing checkers. They drank from bottles in paper bags and wiped sweat from their necks with dirty handkerchiefs. They smoked cigarettes in the hot sun.

I asked if anyone knew anything about the river.

"I bathe in it, that's about all," one man said.

A man with his legs crossed and shiny shins showing said he had nothing to say.

A small man wearing sunglasses who was hunched down on one of the crates said, "You want to know St. Louis you oughtta go down there and take a look at the arch."

"Aw dammit, PeeWee," said a fat man who had suddenly come alive, "they don't want to know about no damn arch. Tell 'em about the rivuh."

PeeWee pointed a weak arm out and said, "Oh, the rivuh. Well, it's right down the street."

Before the night of May 17, 1849, St. Louis boomed as a river city. Trade was carried on down by the river and there were extravagant parties on the anchored steamboats. But on that night in May 1849 the steamboat *White Cloud* caught fire on the wharf. Wind carried the fire to twenty-three other steamboats. One fireman fell through the deck of a steamboat and died.

The fire raced up hills and around street corners, reddening the area, and before it was over more than twenty buildings in the city had been leveled, though many of the buildings along Olive Street, site of the original Lacledes landing, were spared. In recent years there had been efforts at revitalizing the waterfront. Now there were hints of old St. Louis.

What distinguished St. Louis during the steamboat era was its pretty showboats. Auditions were held on the waterfront. Those who couldn't get to Broadway had a chance to dance and sing on the Mississippi. The only showboat that now exists from that grand era is the *Goldenrod*. There were still shows on the boat, but it hasn't moved up and down the river in more than a decade. When the *Goldenrod* was coasting downriver, when the curtains were thrown back and the music struck up, Eileen and Carl Traynor were two of the troupers aboard.

They still lived on the west side of town, in an old red brick home. He had met her in a little Chicago theater when they were both just starting to chase the dream of performing under the lights. Time and opportunity brought them to St. Louis.

Eileen hadn't performed this year because of illness. Carl, a character actor, hadn't performed much this year either. "Roles have been hard to find," he said. He was small and thin and neat. His hair was swept back and parted in a fashion that had been popular in the thirties.

"In the old days they took acting on the boats more seriously," she said.

"Now it's a little hokey," he confessed.

"At one time there were twenty-eight showboats," Eileen said. "Now only the *Goldenrod* is left."

Carl Traynor said most of the shows nowadays were comedies, and even the comedy was pushed so far that it all ended up looking like slapstick.

St. Louis, Missouri

"You deliberately ham it up, but you try not to do it so much that the audience will walk out on you," he explained.

Carl Traynor had a show to do that night. He had been called by the *Goldenrod* this season. It was no major role but it was a role. "There are no small roles," the trouper in him said.

When he couldn't get roles, he had fallen back on his training in accounting. He said he didn't grow bitter when the roles dried up. That was just show business. When the phone rang this season and he was offered a small role, he hustled to the showboat.

Both of the Traynors knew an actress named Blanche Forbes.

St. Louis, Missouri

"She always kept two suitcases packed, right by the door, with her violin," Carl said. There were a lot of fires on the wooden boats in the old days and Blanche Forbes wanted to be ready.

"Well, sure enough," Carl continued, "there was this fire one night and Blanche wakes up and just grabs her suitcases and violin and flew down the back steps." Blanche got away. Now she's living out in California somewhere, a retired actress.

Eileen Traynor had written a little biography of her experiences on the showboats. She brought the neatly typed pages from downstairs — "Just in case you want to look at them."

Carl Traynor, all actorish, stood up quick, patted his hair, took a deep breath, and said, "Well, I got a show to do tonight. Must be going."

After two nights in St. Louis it was time to move on, and on the second morning we prepared to leave. Bill Carroll, captain of the *Huck Finn,* came to the levee to see us off.

Bill Carroll came from Boston and had been traveling the Mississippi River more than forty years. He left Boston to fight in World War II, came to St. Louis after the war, met a woman, fell in love, got married, and stayed: you anchor where the love is. He doesn't take his boat out much now, he said. He lets the up-and-comers take passengers out for the cruises. Every now and then he'll take the stern to show the younger ones the way, to season them.

Bill spoke with a soft Irish accent, and his words had a way of not flying from his mouth. They seemed to curl up first, velvety, and when he talked he fell just short of singing what he said.

The sixty-five-year-old captain wore a navy-blue jacket and brown corduroy pants. His skin was red and reedy and toughened from the river, and his silver hair had the wind in it.

"The river disciplines you," he said slowly, standing on the deck of his boat. "In times of trouble, you either stay on the river and win, or you stay and lose. You just can't suddenly decide to go home."

The captain looked out over the river, seeing what our eyes were too inexperienced to see.

"You'll be okay. Be careful, and whatever you do, don't fall in the river. Give me a call when you get to N'Orleans." That's how he said it — N'Orleans — and it all came out sounding like one word.

A few bystanders stood on the levee watching us, and as we rafted away they waved. Then the captain with the tough red skin started waving, and we lofted our oars skyward. The wind picked up the captain's tie and flung it across his shoulder, and his hair began blowing in the wind as if it were trying to catch the tie. St. Louis disappeared behind the river.

After an hour of rafting from St. Louis, the river traffic began to get heavy. Barges were everywhere. The river now flexed its muscle, spread wider, and the current ran swifter. The raft bounced, riding the rising waves. Slowly, surely, the sky darkened, catching us off guard. The winds picked up and the river began to roll and rain came down furiously. A storm fell upon us, rocking the raft hard. Waves took it up and slammed it back down. I looked at Stan and he looked at me.

"Hold on! Whatever you do, don't fall in."

We kept the rope near our hands just in case. Waves rushed over us and the raft lifted at least ten feet from the rising waves and I imagined two drowned bodies in my vision of horror. Stan hopped about the raft, securing his cameras. The slashing rain dimmed the banks, and nothing was visible except the river and rain. There was nothing to do except hold on and look at each other in fright. It was no longer our raft. The raft now belonged to the storm, and the storm had blackened the sky.

Stan's yellow cushion flew off the raft and landed on top of one of the waves before disappearing behind a line of more waves. And still there was nothing to do, absolutely nothing, except hang on. The waves hit hard, as if someone were throwing them at us. But at last, like a clock winding down, the storm began to ease. Waves still rose angrily and the rain came down hard and cold but the banks began to be visible.

"Let's head over there," Stan yelled, and we used the oars to angle ourselves to the east side of the bank. There, in a little harbor, three men rushed down to help us.

We crashed into the harbor, tossing the men the line, which they grabbed and quickly looped around a pole. "Looks like that storm got to you. It's dangerous out there now," one of the men said as we approached.

Land under foot never felt better. Wet and shaken, we worried about the durability of the raft, wondered where we were.

"Kimmswick, Missouri," one of the men said.

"We better talk about what happened out there," Stan said.

As we made our way into the town of Kimmswick, walking along a back road sided by grass now glistening from the sun that had come after the hard storm, I turned and looked out at the river, aware for the first time of its temperament.

Kimmswick had the old, stilled look you'd expect to see on a Hollywood back lot. Dirt roads wound around the houses. Quilts for sale hung from porch banisters. An afternoon sun reflected from antique tea kettles sitting on the outside windowsills of antique shops. Kimmswick was called "the town that time forgot."

Theodore Kimm, a rich German, founded the town in 1859.

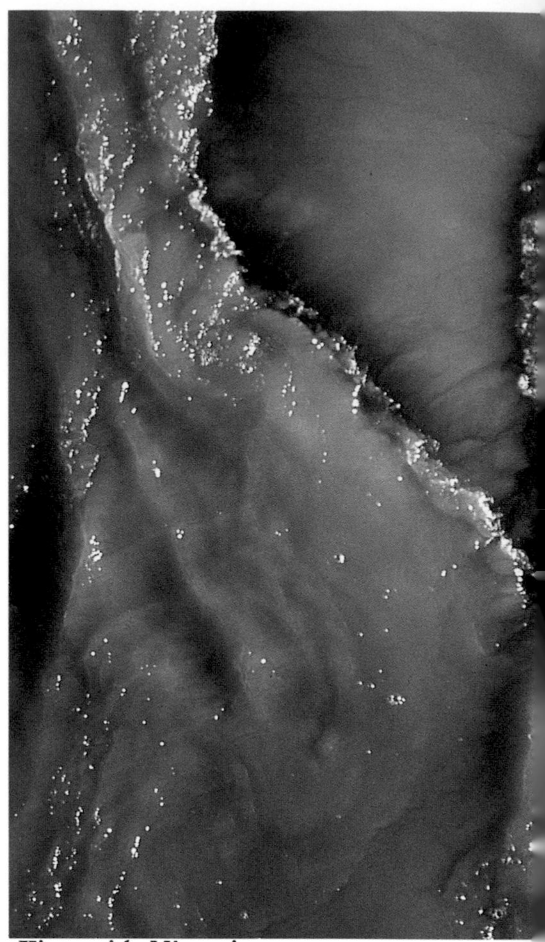

Kimmswick, Missouri

St. Louisans had come there to summer. Years ago there was a flour mill and a brewery and a brick kiln, all gone now.

As we strolled into one of the antique shops, a woman said, "Hi. There's hot coffee beside the door." The sugar cubes were in an elegant blue china bowl next to the coffeepot.

At a restaurant down the road we ordered fried chicken and cole slaw, drank iced tea, finished eating, and just sat watching the candles flicker atop the tables and burn down low. We were tired, storm-weary. Walking back to the river, we crossed a drawbridge and got talking to Bill Knoll, who was fishing.

"Town's seen better days," he said, with what seemed like embarrassment. "We used to have two trains come through here. That was all back in the thirties. We used to have steamboats come through here and stop. All, it was a lively place."

Bill said he was sixty-four, born and raised right here in Kimmswick. A fish nibbled on his hook and he yanked the pole but the fish got away. A few children climbed the drawbridge, laughing down on everyone.

"They put the highway in here and the town started falling apart," Bill said. Folks took fast to the highways that carried them to the big towns with the shopping malls, and that drained the town's commercial district.

Bill used to own a little florist shop on the edge of town. "Me and my brother had it for a long time." Last year when he no longer could look at the cash register at the end of a day and feel good about it, he sold out: gone fishing.

Back at the dock we passed the time talking with the man in charge, Mark Hopkins. Mark was just back from Florida, where he had had a good job on a cruise boat. When his father, Charlie, had gotten sick, he'd come back home to help nurse him and run the dock, because blood is thick.

We asked Mark if we should continue on the raft. "Well," he said, thinking an answer out, "it depends. If you get caught in another storm you might not be so lucky. In early spring like this you can't tell what will happen on the river from day to day."

"What should we do if it starts raining hard and a barge is near and we don't have time to turn?"

"Jump in the river and swim for your life."

Two men had anchored a big cabin cruiser at the dock. They had just come upriver from New Orleans and were on their way to deliver the boat to a doctor in Detroit.

"It's what we do for a living, move boats up and down the river for people," one of the men said. In the early evening they sat up in their cabin, drinking from small glasses, looking out over the river through the misted windows of the cruiser, and watching the rain fall.

Since it was Mother's Day we each called our mother at night from the pay phone that sat in the middle of the dock. Stan talked for ten minutes, I talked for five. Then we paced the dock, back and forth, passing under the light bulb, not minding the chill rising from the river. The rain had stopped but had battered the land enough to wash worms up onto the dock. They squirmed, nearly lifeless.

Lying on the raft, I said, "Stan, did you tell your mom about the storm today?"

"No. No way. Did you?"

"No. I didn't even tell her I was on a raft."

Thirty minutes later, "Stan?"

"Yeah?"

"Do you think we'll make it to New Orleans on the raft?"

"Sure, we'll make it."

It got colder and the river, swollen from the rains, made rushing noises all night. The big cabin cruiser ten yards down the dock from our raft looked warm, secure, comfortable.

In the morning the river was nice and flat and settled under a white handkerchief of a sky. It was as if a brand-new river had been created during the night. We slipped away across the water, smooth enough to lay your head on.

Kimmswick, Missouri

The noon sun sparkled and the ripples turned over and caught the sunlight and the ripples glistened like diamonds skipping across the water. We just rafted.

Of course we'd make New Orleans.

Never been to Paris,
Never been to Switzerland,
Never been to Spain,
To watch it rain,
Never been to Texas,
Not even Corpus Christi,
But I've rafted and rafted,
Upon the Mississippi.

Just singing in the head.

Toward evening the sky began to brood, and then another storm loomed over us and an eerie silence came between Stan and me, as if we knew what was happening but were refusing to acknowledge it. Raindrops fell, then came faster and turned into hail, and Stan yelled, "We got to get off the river. Now!" The waves rose and took the raft up with them again and brought it down just before it was about to tip over.

"I see a little cove," Stan said, his face a wet sponge. It took forty minutes through the wind and rain and against the current to reach the bank. The cove lay behind a thicket of trees. We hopped out and ran through the water up onto the bank and began tying rope around a tree trunk to secure the raft. The rain came harder then and the trees were lashing against one another and the clouds were moving across the sky as if pulled by low, low saxophone music.

"We got off that river just in time," Stan shouted.

There would be no more traveling that day. The storm kept coming, raging. Branches broke from trees and before they hit the ground the wind tore leaves from the branches and scattered them out across the river.

Lightning singed the sky, creating scars of white that appeared, disappeared, then reappeared, but never in the same place. A rumbling noise came up from behind the trees. Could be a train, could be anything. We didn't inspect. Dark began to crawl and we hovered around the lantern. Dinner was served: peanut butter on crackers, a day-old garden salad, candy bars.

We uncorked the bottle of champagne we had bought in St. Louis to celebrate our rafting into New Orleans. But we were thirsty and the champagne, which we drank straight from the bottle, calmed our thirst. It also encouraged singing: oldies but goodies, Motown stuff, sung loudly or sometimes softly, but never on key.

Thunder continued. The rain loosened the earth and the mud under the raft was a cause to worry. So we checked the ropes and retied them, tighter, straining to remember Boy Scout knots.

We fell asleep, an empty champagne bottle standing in the middle of the raft. It was anything but a dream, Stan standing over me two hours later, his eyes wide and glistening. "Get up. Get up. There's a UFO out there, circling the raft." He repeated himself and I opened one eye, then the other, then remembered that we had champagne earlier, and said, "What the hell are you talking about? Lie down." Soon he did, but throughout the night we woke up, checked on each other.

In the morning the river was just shy of calm and covered with a thick mist, like watered-down milk. We pushed the raft out from the mud and sand. Along the riverbanks, trees lay uprooted and dead from last night's storm. Large branches floated by with the current.

The day grew bright and sunny, as still as a romantic idea. Stan sat at the front of the raft, reading, shade falling from the brim of his hat onto the pages of the Hemingway book, his pant legs rolled up, feet in the water, reading and rafting, rafting and reading. Contentment.

I watched for barges, rock dikes.

Then I sat on the edge of the raft, pant legs rolled up, feet in the water.

Overleaf: Chester, Illinois

Stan watched for barges, rock dikes.

Things seemed near, then farther away, then they were gone, over the shoulder. Everything that mattered was connected to the river.

Days got lost like letters in the mail.

"Stan?"

"Yeah?"

"How far to New Orleans?"

"'Bout a thousand miles, maybe a little less."

Cape Girardeau, Missouri, rose on hills, overlooking the Mississippi. We anchored on a strip of bank, and the town overlooked our raft. We waited for a train to go by, then hopped the railroad tracks and trudged across high grass and up a hill. At the top of the hill a man sat in a chair reading a book. When we came upon him we were more startled than he was.

"So you rafting, huh? I watched you anchor." He took off his glasses and closed the book and crossed his legs. He pointed out to the river, downriver from the raft. "When you leave, take good notice of that bit of land out there, that little island. Stay away from it. There's a strange current out there, and a drop-off of about seventy feet. It's a dangerous spot." It was a beautiful piece of advice. "Thank you. Thank you very much."

A man in a store looked at us and asked, "Where y'all headed?"

"New Orleans."

"New Orleans? Those Cajuns catch y'all wearing those wild-ass hats they'll kick your asses." We laughed. "I ain't kidding," he said. We left and checked into the Downtown Motel for showers. After almost two weeks on the raft, sleep at night came quickly on a mattress. Then, in the next moment, I turned my head on the pillow and caught the light streaming past the cheap motel curtains and the light seemed to bring Stan's voice with it: "Hey, come on, get up, let's go." It was 7:00 A.M. I struggled from the bed like a wounded athlete.

We stood out on the balcony, admiring a pleasant morning, glimpsing the river a half mile away. A woman across the alley was planting flowers in her backyard. A small cat followed her wherever she went in the yard.

"Well hi, boys," she said. Her name was Leona Bunch. "Everybody calls me Honeybunch." She said she was eighty years old, a fact that someone had gotten ahold of and run off with to the local newspaper.

"Everybody in town knows my age now. On my birthday they had a picture of me in the paper, and under the picture it said 'Happy Eightieth Birthday, Leona Bunch.' I can't lie about my age now to save my soul."

Her dress was lime green. Nickel-plated earrings hung from her ears. She had removed one of her garden gloves and laid a bare hand across the fence. The cat pawed soundlessly at her ankles.

Leona Bunch told about her volunteer work at the local hospital, St. Francis. By her own telling, she was a gadabout.

"Now we had two people who graduated from the high school last Sunday with straight A's," she said, clearly upset it was just two out of the entire graduating class. "Some get it easily," she said, referring to academics. "Others have to dig from sunlight to dark."

She met her husband when she was attending Southeast Missouri State University, where she studied to be a teacher. "I set my hat for him. That's how I hooked him." She smiled.

She was not amused that we were traveling the river. Too many horror stories had fixed in her mind.

"A towboat turned over last year, right where the Ohio River meets the Mississippi. The cook and captain drowned. They was looking for the bodies for the longest. And they just got the captain out about a month ago."

She patted her attractive auburn hair and said, "How in the world do you keep from the sun out on that raft? You know, over at the hospital we have a lot of people with skin cancer. Catch it from the sun." Her eyes were glued to Stan's neck.

As we walked away she said, in the sweetest voice you ever heard, "I hope you boys don't drown."

As we rafted toward Cairo, Illinois, a hard wind came and knocked a flap from the raft. Stan feared the steel drums underneath the raft were beginning to loosen from the pressure of mud and sand. A barge approached, and our emergency engine would not start. Then, when the barge was far too close for comfort, the engine started at last. The wind didn't let up. We angled the raft to the west bank of the river and wedged it in between a rock dike, then ran the rope up on a hill and tied it around a fallen tree trunk. Stranded, like old times.

We had to find lumber in the nearest town to repair the raft.

We climbed rocks and then a hill and looked out over a big expanse of farmland. Cairo had to be about two miles away, we figured. A man was sitting at the end of the field atop a tractor. We headed off in his direction and when we reached him he climbed down. He was looking at us as if we were buck naked.

"We're on a raft and are having problems. We need to get to a store. Are we near Cairo?"

He turned forty-five degrees and said, "Cairo's over there, a few miles," and quickly got back up on the tractor and motored away, no time for fools.

We headed off in the direction the farmer had pointed. Mud oozed into the holes of my sneakers.

We reached a creek stretching along the expanse of the land, and there was no way to get out to the road without crossing it. We located a log and dropped it across the ten-foot-wide creek. I went first, took three steps, felt myself slipping, so turned and fell backward onto land, caught by Stan. He tried going across, got to the middle, but the log started to slip from the bank and into the creek. He leaped backward onto land.

We returned to the brush and got another log, longer, sturdier. Then I made a mad dash across the log, going too fast to be stylish but landing on solid ground. Stan then repeated my feat. We continued walking. Huck and Jim.

A mile's worth of dirt road brought us to a paved road where we tried hitchhiking. Cars zoomed by as if we were ghosts. A mile later, and across the road, we spotted Vera's Place, really just a house with a sign thrown up over it.

In the darkened barroom a group of five men were sitting around a table, watching cartoons on a television set.

"Anybody here got a car? We need a ride to Cairo. We'll pay."

"How much?" a tall man asked.

"Ten dollars."

Then the man went into a back room and returned with another man, who said, "Say you wanna ride to Cairo?"

"Yeah."

"Ten dollars?"

"Yeah."

"Let's go."

Vernon Hughes's pickup truck rumbled down the road. His thick hands rested on the smooth black steering wheel. He managed the bar with his wife, Vera. I told him we were traveling the river and he said, "Well, I'll tell you something. The river don't mean nothing to Cairo no more. Things are dying here."

It should be a different story, he said. "I mean, heck, this is where the Ohio flows into the Mississippi. You see what I'm saying? Now over in Paducah things are jumping."

But on Friday and Saturday nights, he admitted, a lot of the young ones filed into Vera's Place. "Nowhere else for 'em to go," he reasoned. He pulled into town, took the ten-dollar bill, and said, "Anytime, fellas, anytime."

During a glum and windy afternoon we strolled the streets of Cairo. The town looked tired and slack. Storefronts were boarded up.

Cairo, Illinois

It was a fact that once Cairo was a booming town. Its fall came with the rioting of the sixties. The local police department used to drive a tank through the city's housing project over on Sycamore Street, bellowing the hours of a curfew from a bullhorn.

Down at the riverfront, men sat and watched barges float by. They drank beer from cans. A few kids roamed, shooting rocks from slingshots. Every now and then a couple would stroll by and dab the air with romance.

A large park lay by the river. A man climbed the rocks and met us eye to eye. He held a fishing pole in one hand and a catfish in the other. "I reckon it's a ten-pounder," he said, making his way to his car.

A woman sat on a bench with her arm around the neck of a man. "I'll tell you what happened to Cairo," Karen Henson said, removing her arm from the man's neck. "They took away prostitution and gambling. That's what killed Cairo. And of course the riots didn't help either."

The man who sat next to her was Nick, her newly met and wed husband. Karen explained how the fast marriage had happened, the charm, the surprise of it, still in her voice.

"I was sitting in this bar and he walks in. He comes over to me and sits down without asking and starts telling me his life story, about working up and down the river on the boats, about being down in Florida, about drifting around."

"That's just how it happened," said Nick, whose eyes were bloodshot.

A day later they were in love. A week later they were married. Nick might be gone in a week, a month. That did not seem to be the issue.

"Hey, why don't y'all drop by the apartment tonight," Nick said, hollering the words out as though he were at a Vegas crap table.

"Don't think so," Stan said. "Gotta be moving along."

We walked fifty yards, then finished the trip through the park by racing. I edged Stan out by a good yard.

At a hardware store we bought a piece of wood for the raft. The sky was growing dark, and we figured we'd sleep the night in Cairo and get back to the raft in the morning.

We ate steak sandwiches and sweet-potato pie at a restaurant, then walked the neon-lit streets. In daylight the town had looked dirty and dusty, but at night it seemed almost seductive. It looked cool. Things were sharp and colorful in the dark. Men stood in doorways, in their own shadows, flicked cigarettes, rolled their eyes, looked up and down the street as if waiting for someone. Behind a large bar window, tall men leaned like ser-

Cairo, Illinois

pents over a pool table. Things had that Edward Hopper look, sharp, cool, clean.

But by morning that sharp, cool look was gone and the eyes again noticed the boarded-up buildings. Whatever charm the neon lights had provided was now gone. Dust rose from the curbsides and people walked through it as if it were not there and you knew Cairo was not truly Edward Hopper.

Fred Khourie owned a shoestore in Cairo. He opened the business in 1940, with five hundred dollars and a dogged intention to succeed.

"Business was just great," Khourie said, standing in his shoestore. He pointed to little pictures tacked on the wall. The pictures, taken in the forties and fifties, showed customers jammed inside his store.

"Look at 'em. That's how busy we were. That's right. Even had to turn folks away." He was on the balls of his feet, rocking. "People used to come across the Ohio and Kentucky bridges to shop here. Aw, it was something. This whole street was thriving."

Now many of Fred Khourie's shelves were empty. Up front there was clothing in bins, bargain-basement garments.

It seemed to be mostly pride that kept him in the shoe business. He pointed toward the front of the store where two clerks stood. "They're family. Gotta hire family to keep the overhead down." He told us the mall on the outskirts of town had killed the business district of Cairo, and, personally, he said, he'd rather go down the street and jump off the Ohio River Bridge than step into any mall.

Khourie, short and freckle-faced, lifted a pair of shoes from a box. Stacy Adams, size ten, a church shoe. "Here, try this on," he pleaded, but I told him I would not be needing a pair of Stacy Adams out on the river. "I'm telling you, they'd look nice on you." He rubbed the soles of the shoes with the kind of gentleness usually reserved for the forehead of newborn babies: the life of a salesman.

The next morning we made our way back to the raft, did what repairs were needed, and rafted away. High winds came and we were forced to turn the emergency engine on, but it sputtered, and the wind forced us onto the left bank of the river, where we anchored just beyond the Ohio River Bridge.

We sat on the bank and gazed at the raft, which looked to be shipwrecked. The steel drums underneath were still loosening and we continued to worry.

"Nine hundred miles to go," Stan said.

We threw rocks and broke twigs, and watched the raft bounce up and down with the waves that rolled from the swollen river toward the bank. By the time we had each finished eating a peanut butter and jelly sandwich we figured it would be too dangerous to continue on the raft. In order to make up for lost time we'd better get back on the road. Stan walked up the hill and disappeared over it and went to rent a car.

I sat on a log for an hour, feeling blue about abandoning the raft, but then I finally began to unload our belongings onto the bank: *The Great Gatsby*. A Coleman lantern. A loaf of bread. Sweaters. Two sleeping bags. Tools. The 5 x 7 glossy of Mark Twain, wet, tattered, but still presentable.

Stan returned, keys to the rental car dangling from his hand. We loaded the car, stood atop the hill, stared down at the raft without saying a word. Then two words came from Stan, "Bye, Becky." That's what we had named the raft. Becky Thatcher.

The road map showed the way to Kentucky. Stan threw the road map over his shoulder into the backseat of the car as if it were but a candy wrapper. The mood was quiet.

On the outskirts of town, at the first phone booth, we stopped and I telephoned the Cairo Jaycees, telling them we wanted to donate a shipwrecked raft under the Ohio River Bridge.

"Well," a man on the other end said, "we certainly appreciate it."

"What will you do with it?"

"We'll cut it up, probably use it for firewood in the winter for the poor. Got a lot of poor in Cairo."

Cairo, Illinois

Christmastime without snow lay on these cool Kentucky back roads, and there was a mint smell full of fresh pine and shade and green. Something sweet seemed to land on the tongue as the shade spread everywhere, and the road kept turning and dipping into more fresh pine and mint smells.

Around a turn was a basketball rim with a net hanging still in the Kentucky air. We pulled up to the empty court, got the basketball out of the backseat, and started shooting and listening to the net pop softly. We shot and shot, and sweat spread from our foreheads to our chests. Then the rim and net began to blur against the dusk of evening, and we rode on.

Hickman, Kentucky, was Sunday-evening quiet as we sat in the car at a curb. Riding around town we had seen no motel or inn and got ready to yank the sleeping bags out of the trunk. A couple was sitting on a porch at the end of the street. Stan drove up and leaned his head out the window.

"Hi, we're looking for a motel or inn."

The man rose and came down to the car. He peered inside and a grin spread over his face.

"An inn? Well, I'll tell ya something. Ain't no motels or inns here. You done about reached the *inn* of the world." The grin turned into laughter, ours mixed with his.

We explained we were traveling the river, and he turned to the woman on the porch, introducing her as his wife, and said, "Honey, these two fellas is traveling the river and they need someplace to stay tonight." A thought settled in his mind, and he said, "I reckon that trailer out back is big enough for the both of 'em, ain't it?"

"Sure is," his wife said.

"Y'all got sleeping bags, ain't ya? Well, get 'em and come on."

"No, no, we don't want to impose."

"You ain't imposin'. The trailer's just out back sitting there under the sky. Get the bags. Come on."

We loaded the bags and tossed them in the trailer, then heard Richard's voice sweeping along the backyard. "Y'all wanna see Hickman? Let's go. I'll show you what's to see of it." Everyone piled into the pickup truck. Richard's wife, Jeri, tucked herself into the little space in back of the front seat.

As we rolled up the high hills of the town in the dark warm night, gnats splatted against the windshield. Richard parked on a cliff overlooking the Mississippi River, and everyone climbed out. He walked around the truck to where he could face the river below. When he reached the hood of the truck his wife eased up behind him and put an arm around his waist. "Ain't it beautiful, honey?" she said.

"Sure is."

The town rose on three hills, and the lights from the hills threw beautiful colors onto the surface of the river, and the river caught the light from the homes and threw the lights into the shadows. The sky was elegant, and streaks of light red spread across it. Mark Twain once said that Hickman provided the prettiest view along the river.

I took a step closer to the edge of the cliff and noticed the blue moon that Patsy Cline so tenderly sang about in "Blue Moon over Kentucky." The scene drove me back to the hood of the pickup, where I scribbled notes in the dark, and wondered if I had ever seen a lovelier sight at night in a town. I hadn't.

In 1927 a great flood swept through the river towns along the Mississippi River. Towns were leveled, and bodies were slammed against concrete and buried under waves. Some said that was the death of the American river town. A body count showed 313 dead. The government said the damage was more than $300 million.

"My daddy worked day and night sandbagging the levee," Richard said about the flood.

For the most part, Hickman survived the flood, and time rolled on.

Cruising back down the hill we noticed that the river was still gleaming full of night colors, the moon still blue, but a little of the streak of red in the sky had drifted onto the edge of the moon, scarring it a bit.

Richard was working for Goodyear, and Jeri was attending night school. They had a couple of kids at home. Every twenty yards or so they would comment on the town, its politics and social history.

"Last year was the first time a black man was convicted for killing another black man," Jeri, who had sat on that jury, revealed. Rich was now wheeling through the section of town where most of the blacks lived. "Before that, it was always that if a black man killed another black man he'd get off the hook. The law didn't care. But it was different last year."

Rich rolled around a corner. "Got some rich folks live here in Hickman. Look there at that house." A big rich-looking house, maybe a small mansion, white columns rising in front of it, sat thirty yards away, buffeted on each side by tall trees. We rode down another street and Rich turned satirical, Hickman's Sinclair Lewis: "Hickman's a very religious town. Got twelve churches and thirteen liquor stores."

White lights lay over the street ahead, and about fifty people were gathered outside of a church illuminated by the same lampposts. "Revival. Must be over with now," figured Rich. "Lots of Pentecostals here. You can come down to this neighborhood

Hickman, Kentucky

some nights and if you got a guitar in your arms, you can knock on a door and get yourself a revival going. Ain't that right, honey?"

"Yep. Sure is."

"Y'all must be hungry," and before we answered, Rich was heading for the local diner.

We slid into a booth, ordered fish. Everyone knew Rich and Jeri.

"These fellas is traveling the river. They just got to Hickman," he told everyone. Their eyes set on us, folks offered greetings. While we were waiting on the meal, our talk invariably turned to the river.

A woman sitting in the next booth over spoke up. "Now, last year a man and his wife and their little girl went out on the river. They stayed out there too late and when they started to come back upriver it was dark, couldn't see a thang. They never saw the barge that hit 'em, I'd figure. No way. The husband and wife were fished from the river. The little girl's still out there. Probably hung in some bush under the river or something. Poor thang."

A man said, "Hey, Rich, you tell 'em what happened couple years ago, about ol' John, who was traveling downriver, headed for New Orleans?"

"Oh yeah," Rich said. "Naw, I didn't tell 'em that one."

So the man did it himself. "Well, ol' John, his boat breaks down, right here in Hickman, and he gets out to fix it and didn't know how to fix the damn thing, so he just unloaded his boat and been here ever since. Built him a little place down by the river. Don't say much to folks. Kinda strange."

After the meal we went back to Rich and Jeri's, a one-floor home with plenty of room.

"Hey, y'all, look at this," Rich said, pulling a ten-foot-high American flag from behind the door, beaming. He said he liked to stick it out on the holidays and just listen to it flap against the wind.

The kids, Lori and Lynn, showed off family photos until the wall clock struck eleven. "Time for bed, gotta go to school tomorrow," their mom announced.

Rich walked us out to the trailer. That Kentucky mint smell still hung in the air. "What a night," Rich said, his head thrown back and his chest almost parallel to the sky.

He said good night and disappeared under the porch light into the house. We climbed into the trailer, flicked on flashlights to make out the interior.

"Stan?"

"Yeah?"

"What nice folks."

Lori Scarbrough, Hickman, Kentucky

"It's a great country, man."

About a minute later, which turned out to be six hours later, Rich's voice floated through the air and through the screen windows of the trailer. "Hey, y'all, let's go get some breakfast." He was standing in the front yard, smiling, a man ready to get out there and go at the world.

Sunny-side up eggs, crisp bacon, let the day begin. Rich needed only black coffee at the restaurant we had driven to. He said a hello over his shoulder to everybody in the place, then rose, as if on cue, and slipped back behind the counter, where he lifted the coffeepot, returned to the dining area, and filled everyone's cup. Everyone kept chattering, hardly noticing him. The waitresses said nothing. It was strange to see, and yet charming. Then Rich lit out for work, and we rode back into town and walked along the streets. They were mostly empty. A man leaned against a giant cola sign as if waiting for the world to end, or change direction, or do something.

A police car rolled by slowly and the officer behind the wheel craned his neck slowly and eyeballed us. I had seen that slow look before and knew he would be back. It took two minutes, just long enough for the U-turn at the corner.

He parked his car across the street and picked up his hand radio and said something into it. He sat a couple of minutes, tapping his fingers on the steering wheel. He picked up the radio again, then, after talking into it for a few moments, got out of the car. As he neared us, I impulsively shoved a piece of ID at him. He looked at it, then said, "I already checked the car out. Y'all okay. Been having some problems around here. The pharmacy right over there was burglarized couple weeks back. Come on round here, take a look." He guided and we followed, around the side of the pharmacy, stopping in back of it.

"I came around here," the officer explained, the need to tell the story once again seizing him, "and the burglar jumped out at me. We wrestled. Boy, I'm telling you we wrestled too. Anyway, he took off yonder, just flyin', gone."

We retraced our steps back to the street, and bid Officer Johnnie Shell good-bye. Before we reached the car, he said, "Tell ya what, you want to take a picture of one of Hickman's finest, well, I wouldn't mind one bit." He put his hands on his holster and spread his feet apart, straightened his back, and assumed a Gary Cooper pose. Stan clicked. Twice. The officer then walked away from the spot where he'd been standing. And just like that, he was no longer Gary Cooper, but just another small-town cop.

Along the road by the river, we made a right, went up a hill, and came to the Hickman County Courthouse. It was an old, lovely courthouse, brick with white trim.

Hickman, Kentucky

(Old buildings like that one sat in the river towns like antiques. But there are enough stories about such buildings being leveled for parking lots and modern buildings to cause one to ache, to wonder why people rush so fast to tear at that which has aged so gracefully.)

Two yard men worked around the edges of the manicured lawn. A man and his wife sat in the front seat of their pickup. They had come to get their fishing licenses.

"Last thing I need is to be fishing and have some ranger guy come charging out the bushes trying to catch me fishing without a license," he said. "Courthouse opens at nine. I'll be on the river fishing by ten." His wife sat quietly, sewing on a piece of cloth. They were the first ones in the courthouse.

Inside, elegant wood doors had names beautifully stenciled on them. A walnut staircase rose three flights, and the sun pouring through the tall windows highlighted the fine wood grain of that staircase. A court worker said there would be no court that day, so we went to see the empty courtroom. Wide doors swung open and the courtroom, silent, all wood, reminded me of the kind of courtroom Spencer Tracy and Frederick March battled in in *Inherit the Wind.* An old, relaxed, almost lazy-looking courtroom. No need to rush in a courtroom like that.

Stan dashed up and sat in the judge's high chair. He leaned forward, a serious look on his face, and mimicked a judge.

"Mr. Prosecutor, what do you base your evidence on? And for the sake of the jury, please be precise and get to the point."

I assumed the pose of a DA and crossed the courtroom slowly, professionally. I faced the judge, then turned to the jury, and fancied an aristocratic southern voice.

"Your honuh, ladies and gentlemen of the jury. What we have here is a travesty of justice, perpetrated by one man for the sole reason of ruthlessness. I will prove to you, far beyond a reasonable doubt, that my client is innocent and has become the victim of an evil witch-hunt by the powerful people who rule our quiet little town."

Stan laughed, and I said, "Your honuh, may I please have a little respect from the bench?"

The doors swung behind us as we left, and their creaking didn't cease until we had reached the bottom of the stairs.

Some in town had spoken of "the old river man," Willie Gaston, and urged us to go see him. We found his house later in the day in between a few other homes and sitting on the second tier of town hills. An awning shaded the porch. I knocked hard on the front door and there was no answer, so Stan went around the back and knocked, but still no answer. From across the yard, a big woman came out of a house. There was a green-and-white

Overleaf: Hickman County Courthouse

rag tied around her head. Two little children followed her out of the house.

"You lookin' for Willie?"

"Yes, ma'am."

"He should be in there. You gotta knock hard. He's hard of hearing. And sometimes he gets his days and nights mixed up. You know, sleeping during the day, awake at night, like that. So he could be sleeping still."

Ten minutes later, just as the knocking began to suggest pounding, he opened the door and turned his head sideways, so an ear could face the screen door and us.

"Yeah? What you want?"

I told him we were traveling the river and wanted to talk to him about his life, and he said, "Well, come on in."

Willie Gaston

In the mid-1890s, when Mark Twain was taking off on world-wide journeys, Willie Gaston was working on the Mississippi River as a roustabout. He traveled with a small bag and the clothes on his back, kept his money in his shoes and sometimes under the brim of his hat. Willie Gaston never had a birth certificate, but as far as he could recall he was 107 years old.

"I was born in Mississippi and left home when I was twelve years old. I was walking down a road and a white man stopped me. He say, 'Can you work?' I said yeah and he hired me. I started out making a penny a day. I milked a lot of cows. Stayed on the plantation until I was twenty-three years old." He left to ride and work the boats going up and down the river. "I went from Cairo down to the Gulf of Mexico."

Mostly Willie loaded cargo and scrubbed decks. The times were rough, full of hellfire, and a man, he said, had to watch his back. "I handled 'em on the river and anywhere else. I was mean as a man could be. I'm comin' clean with you, you see, 'cause I'm going to meet my maker soon. I'm a southerner and I don't want to get anything mixed up."

When he was unsure of fully hearing a question he would place an open palm to his ear, turn his face to the floor as if listening for a cavalry, and say, "Say that again."

There was a white handkerchief in his back pants pocket, a red-banded straw hat on the windowsill, a dozen or so pictures of relatives atop the television set.

There was a sister who lived down in Mississippi. "She's old, like me. I don't expect I'll ever see her again."

His life was full of travel and mayhem, but there was romance, even if there was a price to pay for it. He took a bullet in the side for a woman named Lil. He had gone to pick her up in Cairo, Illinois, and stood at the bottom of some steps yelling her name.

"I was on Fourteenth Street. I said, 'Lil, come on, let's go.'"

There was a commotion, a struggle, and he saw a friend of his hitting Lil. "I said, 'Jim, turn that woman loose. Turn that woman loose, Jim.'"

Jim did not turn Lil loose. Instead, he turned and fired a gun at Willie Gaston, the bullet from the .45 landing in his side. The bullet and shock of it all sent Willie fleeing down the street, bleeding. He finally fell to the pavement like pieces of thrown clothing.

"When I woke up in the hospital, Lil was right there by my side," he said, his eyes gone soft.

He came to Hickman about fifty years ago, got off down at the river, and found a job working for a woman named Mrs. Tyler. Took care of the chickens, did yard chores, a man Friday. When he could no longer work, when all the work had been worked out of his little body, he went to apply for Social Security. He stood in line at the courthouse and was turned away because he didn't have a birth certificate.

"I'd tell 'em they didn't hand out birth certificates when I was born." He'd go back every Wednesday.

"They'd say, 'Willie, what you want, boy?'"

"And I'd say, 'I want my money. I want what's coming to me.'" He kept going back, an old man walking down the road, alone, to the courthouse. Sometimes they would call the police and the police would drive Willie back home. Finally some city agency intervened, and that is how he began to get his Social Security checks. "Lord have mercy," he yelled, recalling the victory, kicking up a leg.

The Hickman police had made peace with Willie Gaston. Every so often one of the officers rode up the hill to check on him. Johnnie Shell, the officer who'd ID'd us earlier that morning, had stopped by the other day.

There was a small garden out in back of the apartment where collard greens and tomatoes grew in the gentle wind. He didn't get out to the garden that day. But it was nice to have a thing like a garden to lean to, something that tugged at the soul, touched it.

He walked us to the screen door and said, "Do me a favor. Don't forget me. Remember me. Remember Willie." Stan caught the screen door in the wind, letting it close softly.

We knew we'd be leaving by evening so we went to the florist and bought flowers for Jeri, Rich's wife. The woman at the florist asked whom the flowers were for. The question seemed strange. "For Mrs. Jeri Scarbrough," and before I could ask her why she wanted to know she said, "Jeri will just love this mix."

When we got back to Rich and Jeri's, there was no one home, so we sat in the swing on the front porch and swung away an

Tiptonville, Tennessee

hour. The crinkly green paper that concealed the flowers on my lap made *hush hush* sounds. Then Jeri came home.

"Aw, guys, y'all didn't have to do this," and she held the flowers to her chest.

Soon Lynn and Lori came home and we all sat out in the backyard. We shot baskets through the rim that hung in the backyard, Stan and Lynn against Lori and me. Lori, a leftie, hit the game-winning basket, from the corner, fifteen feet out. Rich pulled into the driveway, grinning like the county sheriff. Lori said she had a spelling bee to go to back at school so she dashed into the house to change.

"What's the next stop?" Rich asked.

"Probably Memphis."

"Aw, I wish y'all'd have a chance to go to Nashville." He loved Nashville, went there with his wife after they were married, saw all those high-stepping country singers at the Grand Ole Opry.

"Saw *Lowrreeettuuh Lynnnn,*" he said, grinning, letting the name grow in his mouth, wanting Nashville all over again.

Stan walked to the car, opened the trunk, brought out the Coleman lantern, and handed it to Rich. "Naw, fellas, I can't take this. No way. Come on." We insisted, and he took it.

Lori came out of the house, pretty in a pink dress. She's not sweet sixteen yet but one day soon she will land there, and when she does, she will land as gracefully as a butterfly does upon a blade of grass.

"We'll miss everyone," I said, and Rich said, "But not as much as we'll miss y'all."

The mother and daughters of the family hugged us, and the father and son gave good handshakes.

The last we saw of them as they stood there waving was Lori's pink dress, which seemed to get smaller and brighter at the same time. She was standing next to her father, a good man who kept a huge American flag behind the front door.

There was something serene and uninterrupted about the face, and in the voice, a cadence that came from the throat, lush, almost tropical, as if he had spent a part of his youth on an island, Jamaica perhaps. It was just the fine southern accent.

He was born in Atlanta, Georgia, the son of a preacher, and given his father's name — Martin Luther King — and in time took the same occupation as his father. He studied at Morehouse College, then went east to Boston University to study for a doctorate.

Back in Atlanta, he had his own church, and when he preached, his words seemed to settle on the marrow in the bones. He knew big words but his congregation didn't mind, because he used them with qualifiers, where they made sense, where they practically explained themselves. They knew he was scholarly, but he still liked collard greens and corn bread; he was still down-home. A natural leader, they said, as they swayed back and forth in the pews, humming, fanning themselves, amen-ing this and amen-ing that.

Martin Luther King, Jr., eased from the pulpit and went into the streets, to lead old black women in straw bonnets and cotton dresses and old black men in double-breasted suits, to protest and to boycott a segregated nation, to talk of debts owed and opportunities denied.

They were sprayed with firehoses, yanked into paddywagons, knocked on the head. King didn't mind going to jail, and went guided by Thoreau's dictum: "Under a government which imprisons any unjustly, the true place for a just man is also a prison."

He crisscrossed the nation, going from southern city to northern city, from farmland to ghetto, quarterbacking the civil rights movement, gaining a yard here, a yard there, sometimes sustaining a five-yard loss, then preparing new game plans in the night, in segregated hotel rooms.

On a hot August day in 1963 he looked out over a crowd of more than two hundred thousand gathered near the Washington Monument and said, "I have a dream." He told them his dream, and his voice seemed to lift them up and then set them back down, collectively, soft as violets hitting earth. When they landed they seemed to have his dream in them, and his arm was outstretched over them, blacks and whites. They cried. Some remembered him from Selma, Birmingham, Atlanta. They said his reach was great, and they knew he'd do great things.

Fifteen months later he went to Oslo to accept the Nobel Peace Price, the youngest man in the history of the award to receive it.

But all the while it was a dangerous journey upfield. He knew it and his aides knew it. A crazed woman had rushed toward him once in New York City and stabbed a pen into his chest. He survived. The doctors said a sneeze would have killed him. Some saw his survival just short of a miracle, knew he was blessed; someone special, they said.

Death frightens everyone. He rationalized it, accepted it, even once, envisioning his own funeral, gave advice to whoever would read the eulogy: "Say that I was a drum major for justice. Say that I was a drum major for peace. That I was a drum major for righteousness. And all of the other shallow things will not matter. I won't have any money to leave behind. I won't have the fine and luxurious things of life to leave behind. But I just want to leave a committed life behind."

In the first week of April 1968, Martin Luther King, Jr., checked into the Lorraine Motel in Memphis to lead a rally in support of sanitation workers striking because of unequal wages. It was tense, and city officials debated whether they should allow a march. Finally they okayed it.

On the evening before the rally, on his way to a dinner engagement, he stepped out onto the balcony of the motel, took a few steps, smelled the air. Bullets shot into his neck and slammed his body against the wall. His aides down below ducked for cover, then scrambled to his side. He lay in a pool of blood, his life slipping by the moment. He died under the lights of an operating room.

From the flophouse across the street someone had seen a figure fleeing, getting in a dirty white mustang and taking off. America began to reel. There were riots, blood on the land. Six dead in Washington, D.C., four dead in Los Angeles. A kid lay slain on a streetcorner in Tampa, his throat slashed open.

Lyndon Johnson, already haunted by the demons of Vietnam, pushed his big Texan body through the White House, sorrow-filled. "America shall not be ruled by the bullet," he said. The hooves of the National Guard were heard up and down the streets of urban America. Flames shot from rooftops and there was widespread looting. The FBI was chasing the assassin.

Robert Kennedy, at the time a New York senator running for the presidency, stood before a mostly black crowd in Indianapolis, in the cold rain, and told them in a quavering voice that King was dead. An aide held an umbrella over his head as he quoted Aeschylus: "In our sleep pain that cannot forget falls drop by drop upon the heart, and in our own despair, against our will, comes wisdom to us by the awful grace of God."

They buried the young preacher in Atlanta. The known and the unknown attended the funeral. Jacqueline Kennedy was ushered in through a side door. A cart with two mules carried his body to its final resting place.

James Earl Ray, at one time identified as drifter, riverboat cook, janitor, master of disguises, was being sought as the assassin. He was also an escaped convict. He eluded the FBI, running from the southwest to Canada, leaving the scantest clues behind in flophouses and whorehouses and cheap motels. When he stepped off a plane in London on his way to South Africa, Scotland Yard was waiting. They arrested him with the smoothness of a bank transaction.

We rode into Memphis, along the river, then parked the car. Stan went to take pictures. I began a walk over to the Lorraine Motel, curious, wanting to see it.

Before I reached it a young woman, about twenty-five, said, "Hi, you want a southern girl?" I said no and kept walking and when I looked back over my shoulder she was staring at me as if we had known each other from high school. Other women were loitering in the shade of the motel, and I saw two others in the lobby. A motel worker told me that the Lorraine mostly caters to prostitutes and their dates.

I looked up at Room 306, the room where King slept the night before he was shot. This was the place, depending on whom you listened to, where a dream was either born or died.

Calvin Brown, standing in the parking lot, described himself as an unofficial tour guide. He escorted me up the steps to Room 306. There was a dirty plastic wreath on the railing and a stone plaque that said, THEY SAID TO ANOTHER, BEHOLD, HERE COMETH THE DREAMER . . . LET US SLAY HIM . . . WE SHALL SEE WHAT BECOMES OF HIS DREAMS. GENESIS 37: 19–20.

Brown opened the door and we stepped inside and my eyes went around the room slowly: pictures of King were tacked on the walls. On one of the pictures someone had scrawled, "I Love You, Martin." A bible lay open in a far corner. An unlit candle sat in a candle holder. Books lined a shelf. Three pairs of women's shoes were under a glass case. It turned out that the shoes belonged to the wife of Walter Bailey, the motel manager. His wife had died on the day King was shot: shock, heart attack. The

Memphis, Tennessee

shoes, Brown explained, were something of a legacy, as were the books with which her husband had lined the walls. The authors ranged from John Steinbeck to W. Somerset Maugham to Martin Luther King, Jr., himself.

There was a visitors book atop the glass case. Visitors had come from California, Japan, Russia, the world.

"The middle-class blacks always tried to claim King, but he was for the underdog, the sanitation worker, the prostitute," Brown said, leaning on the glass case. "And maybe, just maybe, the prostitutes knew that and that is why they keep doing their business here. If it wasn't for them the Lorraine would have to close."

There had been attempts over the past several years to turn the Lorraine into a shrine honoring King. A Lorraine Civil Rights Museum Foundation was formed but it never could raise money. One time, professional basketball players came in and played a game to raise money. The venture lost money instead. The Lorraine Civil Rights Museum Foundation was broke.

Rooms at the motel went for seventeen dollars a night. The big suite atop the manager's office went for twenty-six.

Calvin Brown checked in ten years ago. He had come up from Mississippi, where he said he was a record producer. He had a room at the Lorraine and served as tour guide and walked the parking lot in the daytime with glossy pictures of King in his hand that he sold for one dollar. As tour guide, he got a special rate on his room.

The next evening I returned with Stan, wanting him to see the inside of Room 306. Calvin Brown was in the parking lot wearing a red-checkered suit and straw hat and standing in patent-leather shoes.

"The keys are lost," he said, when I asked him to take us up to the room. His voice was sharp. Then he said, "Let the tourists come here for themselves. They don't need to see pictures." He was embarrassed for the motel. We walked up the steps and stood on the outside of the room and Stan looked at the dirty wreath and said, "This is a shame."

A man walked with a high-heeled woman past the room, and, for a moment, they were caught in the lone glow of the light bulb above the doorway.

Back down in the parking lot, Calvin Brown, in the softest of voices now, said, "You know something, this is the only city where two kings ever died." The rock and roll king, Elvis Presley, died on August 16, 1977. He had been taking too many pills and the pills clashed with one another and his heart gave out.

Brown walked into the lobby and sat down between two women. As we walked past the lobby I peered in at him. I wanted to say something like "Keep the faith, Calvin," but the words died in my throat.

Back at the Peabody Hotel that night we took the elevator to the roof and stepped into the soft night.

Years ago big bands — Tommy Dorsey's, Benny Goodman's — used to play on this roof. Ladies in pretty dresses leaned on the soft shoulders of gentlemen, and the fine fragrance of the women must have lifted up the air.

Over in a corner a couple stood talking, his hands around her waist. He was trying to explain something to her, and it sounded as if she did not quite understand. Maybe they needed Benny Goodman or Tommy Dorsey.

Down below, Memphis beat on. Across a stretch of buildings the river could be seen, breathing in and out.

If you love barbecued ribs you will walk a country mile to get a plate of them. As it turned out we had to walk only across the street from the Peabody Hotel to reach Charlie Vergos's Rendezvous. It was lunchtime and a pretty day to be in Memphis. A bank clock showed the temperature to be eighty-eight.

Halfway down the alley a big yellow sign poked out, advertising the place. It was quiet walking down the steps. A group of men were sitting around a table and the rest of the restaurant was empty. One of the men leaned back and stopped us on the steps with his voice, "Sorry, fellas, closed today."

I told him we were traveling the river, on assignment, and had heard that his place was the best place along the river to get a good plate of ribs, and all we wanted to do was pay for one of those plates.

"Well, come on down, and I'll see what I can do," he said, flattered.

Even though the place was not open for business, two cooks were laying down slabs of ribs onto the charcoal-blackened grill, smoke rising into their eyes.

Civil War mementos — rifles, hats, pictures — hung from one brick wall. Another wall was decorated with black-and-white photos of old-time Hollywood stars.

Charlie Vergos got the idea for his rib house, he explained, when he was in Paris during World War II, dashing in and out of bars and cafés. "I said, hell, I can do the same thing back home."

Memphis, Tennessee

Rib Festival, Memphis, Tennessee

So after the war he returned to Memphis, worked and saved some money, and, in 1948, bought a little place. Business went well. He had created his own special barbecue sauce. Then one night while he was at home the place burned to the ground. They never exactly pinpointed how the fire started. "Total destruction," he said, setting a plate of ribs before us.

He did not know what he was going to do after the fire. There was a man in town named Abe Plough, a wealthy man who always had admired Charlie Vergos's drive and hustle. On the morning after the fire, Abe Plough sent his driver over to the burned building with a message for Charlie: "Put your bills in a sack and get ready to go back to work."

"That's all he said," Vergos remembered.

Abe Plough financed Vergos's venture and he was back with the barbecued ribs, and that is why, on a wall, there was a life-size picture of Abe Plough, the businessman sitting at his desk, hands crossed.

"He'd come in here to eat but always insisted on paying for his own meal," Vergos said about Plough. "Couldn't give him a free meal."

Vergos runs the restaurant with his son. On some nights the line stretches up the alley and out to the street. He's won several barbecue contests in the city.

We ate the ribs like prisoners on the lam, the sauce running down our chins. There were creased linens to wipe our mouths with. Stan said, "Goddamn," and so did I, because that's how good the ribs were. Big Charlie Vergos stood over us, laughing. "Yes, sir," he bellowed, "we take our ribs seriously here in Memphis. Don't come here talking about ribs on the East Coast. We won't stand for it."

In Memphis on Friday nights the place to be is Beale Street. There were clean clothes on my body and baby powder on my chest, and I stepped quickly to keep up with Stan. The night was warm as fresh milk, and Beale Street was jammed. Sailors strolled looking for romance, pieces of neon reflecting in their patent-leather shoes.

Old street musicians blew on harmonicas and tapped on organs and kicked their feet up off the cement. Fingers popped. Heads nodded in the shadows like bruised plums. Young women posed like fashion models. The breeze from the river climbed backs, kissed necks. Ice was crushed, doused with fruit flavors, instant snow cones.

A bigger-than-life statue of W. C. Handy was set back off the street, at the entrance of a small park. Little kids ran circles around ol' Handy, who not only played Beale Street in Memphis, but Market Street in St. Louis and Broadway in New York City.

Memphis, Tennessee

The night took us into W. C. Handy's, a Beale Street jazz club. The atmosphere was cool, and there was the low and almost secretive chatter of a speakeasy. Cigarette smoke hung in the air like spider webs. A ceiling fan twirled. Black marble-topped tables shined.

Drinks came in old-fashioned jelly jars. There were thin bottles of hot sauce on the tables with which to smother the catfish. The Club Handy Blues Band — a drummer, a sax player, a guitarist — began to warm up. The sign at the door had advertised that a Ruby Wilson would be the featured vocalist.

The blues. Aging men in sunglasses, hurt women leaning on staircases, lovers fighting, narcotics, stormy weather.

Ruby Wilson, big, dressed in black, smiling wickedly through blood-red lipstick, emerged from the shadows and let the applause lead her to the stage. She broke right into "C. C. Rider." Belting from the gut, her hands on her big hips, men growling, her voice going low enough to pick up gravel and sling it, sassy lady.

Somebody cried, "Tell it like it is, Ruby bab*eeee,*" and someone else let loose with a long *Yeessssss,* as if they had just been released from jail.

She sang "Georgia on My Mind," and dabbed at beads of sweat on her forehead with a red handkerchief. She seemed on the verge of tears.

Then she started strutting again, rumbling like a train in the dark, powerful, soulful. She took Billie's "Lover Man" and sent the lyrics to the rear of the club and then demanded they come back, only so she could send them out again. At the end of that number, the crowd in a blues frenzy, Ruby Wilson, with sweat dripping, leaned and said, "Hey y'all, this here ain't nothing but a party down here on Beale Street. In Memphis, Tennessee, U.S.A."

A couple of years back Ruby Wilson landed a guest-starring role on the television series "On the Mississippi." Many in Memphis thought she was going to leave Memphis and go Hollywood. But she stayed: she was Memphis.

The last line of her last song of the night went like this: "You can have my husband, but please don't mess with my man."

By 1:00 A.M., the characters on Beale Street seemed to have multiplied. Street vendors in the night hawked trinkets, gadgets, and pictures of Elvis.

Memphis is the blues and soul, and cotton too. The Memphis Cotton Exchange, on Union Street, operates now as a deference to history. It is no longer a place of intense activity as it was forty years ago, when cotton merchants came to town to pass along information on the crop and do their trading.

On this morning, just a few men were there. One leaned on a wood stool and stared up at a green chalkboard through bifocals. The market figures on the chalkboard were apt to be a day or two behind, a merchant explained, but no one made a fuss.

The Cotton Exchange, said cotton merchant Calvin Turley, was now a place to come and recall what got away. A scent of the old days lingered, like the smell of a pipe in a gentleman's study. An old man walked by, his trousers held up by suspenders, his head covered with a straw hat. Attitudes lingered too.

Some still contend cotton is king here in Memphis, but it was no longer true. Cotton was king over in Texas now. And merchants in Memphis said the cotton industry ails the way the steel industry does.

"Cotton is now a game of international fluctuations," said Turley, who at thirty-five is one of the youngest cotton merchants on Cotton Row. Turley had a computer in his office, printouts of market figures at his elbow. Many try to get in the cotton game, he said, and don't last. With competition, "there's very little room in the cotton industry for mediocrity."

It used to be enough to know the crop, know a field, have contacts in town, know how to best ship your bales downriver, know how long it would take. "Now a merchant would do well to know some foreign languages," Turley said. Exports, imports; know the market.

Most of the buildings along Cotton Row were sepia-colored. Men in white smocks dashed up and down the streets with cotton samples in cardboard boxes to deliver to merchants. The river still flowed right by the buildings.

Some of the names on the buildings recalled an old era: Patton Brothers Cotton Merchants, Pursell & Culver Company. Boys used to hawk the *Saturday Evening Post* up and down Cotton Row.

For every cotton merchant with a fine cigar in his shirt pocket and a gallon jug of mountain water in his office, there was a cotton runner down on the street, an errand man, a front-row person sort of guy. It has always been a menial job. That never meant you had to dress down for it.

William Shipp, whom everyone called Pluto, was a Cotton Row runner. He leaned on a box of cotton, in a maroon pair of dress shoes — "They's Stacy Adams" — creased gray slacks, a red windbreaker, and enough jewelry for three people. The quarter stuck in each ear was for the parking meter for his boss's car. He had worked for F. G. Barton Cotton Company more than twenty-five years.

"Born right here in Memphis," he said. "Cotton Row used to be different. Used to be more businesses, more cafés."

Pluto, Memphis, Tennessee

FESTIVAL
LONDON
Hard Rock
NEW YORK

Cotton Exchange, Memphis, Tennessee

He was divorced, with one daughter. "Don't see her much," he said, not explaining why.

He'd known hard times on Cotton Row, but he'd been around too long to leave.

"I was in a bar and this guy I knowed said I owed him some money, which I did. Well, I paid him and he said I owed him some more, which I didn't. I walked out the door and came on down the street, right to this corner. When I got up here I just then did turn around a little. The guy bust me over the head with a metal pipe. I laid up in the hospital for three months."

The man had work to do, and as he walked away the taps on the heels of his shoes clicked against the cement. Someone from across the street yelled, "Hey, Pluto, where you headed?"

"Up the way," he yelled back across the street. He was now far enough away where the clicking of the taps could no longer be heard.

On the afternoon of the next day we packed what few things we had, walked over to Charlie Vergos's rib house, bought ribs for the road, headed for the levee, and hauled on out of Memphis. By the time stars appeared in the sky, the ribs had been eaten.

There is, about most northern cities, a fast pace, as if the people are trying to keep up to the beat of a 45 rpm record. The southern city has a slower, more languid pace; things are as easy as the movement of a 33 rpm record.

In Helena, Arkansas, a woman on the street said, "We had a boy here once, went off to travel the river. He started up there in Minnesota too. When he got back down here to Helena, though, he spent a night with his girlfriend. Never did get back on the river."

There were still dirt roads, their dust kicked up by cars turning on them. Weather-beaten shacks sat back from the roads; cars three decades old sat at the sides of the shacks as if their time would come again. A mangy dog raced under a car, then chased little kids, barking at their heels.

The river, up over the railroad tracks, was running high and fast. A year back, a man in town said, they pulled a man out of the river in Helena. They opened his wallet to check for identification, found out he was a first-class lifeguard.

We took a room at a big rooming house off Main Street, sat on the front porch, watched cars go by, listened to bugs cry out, and watched the night age.

The next morning as we were going through town, on our way out, we saw a gentleman leaning back on a chair against a building trimmed in soft shades of pink and blue. It was a contrast to the rest of the town. I got out of the car and headed his way and that caused him to go inside.

"I got nothing to say to no reporter," he said.

"I'd like to know about the town history. I bet you been living here a long time."

"All my life."

"Then I'd like to talk to you."

He looked to his left, then to his right, as if we were being watched. "Well, I reckon I can talk for a little spell. Come on in." I motioned to Stan.

His hands were long and thin like the hands of a concert pianist. He had never played piano, but Walter Powell had decorated some fine homes in Helena, where he had come in the twenties. "The river was frozen the year I came here," he said.

His first job was unloading freight off the river. But soon he became interested in decorating and taught himself a few things about elegance, about colors.

"Wore suits to work every day. Shirt starched. Suit nice and pressed. I decorated the homes of the rich people."

It was hard to imagine a black man in the thirties and forties and fifties moving around this town as a decorator. He probably was mostly a painter, and maybe he painted with pastel colors, treating everything as a fine-eyed artist might. So, a decorator, in his own mind, was what he was.

These days Walter Powell traveled a new road. He wore old work clothes and a raffish hat and waited for someone to knock who might need some decorating, or just plain housework. The years had caught him and he no longer went charging out of the house under the morning sun as he once had.

He had set up shop alone, though that had not been the original plan. He was supposed to start up a business with two friends, and the business was to be housed in this one-floor building, which was the size of a huge loft. The friends backed out of the business deal at the last minute and Powell was left alone. "I got my clothes and moved in here anyway," he said. He had brought his tools with him.

Scrap was in one corner. A huge cola sign looked down from one wall. Tin cans sat, draped by sheets of white canvas. Ladders leaned on walls. Things looked begun but unfinished.

Truth was, if someone had knocked on the door there'd have been doubts whether Powell could have gone and done a job. There were physical ailments. The eyesight was not what it once was. But never kill a man's reason for being.

There was a little stove in the back and a little bunk bed in back of the area with the stove; a naked light bulb showed off the place. "Got everything a man could ever need right here."

He had rigged up his own heating system, and, while he conceded that it had been known to collapse, he had gotten by in the winters so far, and he'd go into the next without fear.

Walter Powell, who never married, had honey-brown skin and eyes that shined like black pearls.

I told him that the town reminded me of someplace that had always been safe, easy to live in, and he said, "Oh no, no. A terrible thing happened in this town." The knot in his throat was the size of a child's knuckle: his Adam's apple was moving up and down.

"Back in 1926 they took a black man out of one of the stores here in town. They said he had touched some white girl. Now, no one ever proved this. They took that boy and tied him up with a rope and drug him around town. I saw it all with my own eyes. They took him up on a hill, right by the river. They tied him up to a tree. Then they threw a match on him and burned that boy to *death*."

His voice whispered. "They told all the blacks to stay in the house for several days. Myself, I slept with an axe by my bed. I remember a friend of mine who lived outside of town. He was a black man, a well-to-do black man. They told him he better not come in town."

He said there were never any arrests. "If anyone said anything, they would have been killed. Now, that's what happened in this town, right here. A terrible thing." Believing that event had scarred the town forever, he said, "Won't be long before the town's just gone; won't be long at all."

It started to rain, and we heard raindrops pelt the roof. Sounds echoed down into the exposed pipes in the ceiling. The noise was like the ringing of very little bells.

As we left, walking through the raindrops, Walter Powell said, "If y'all ever down this way again, stop in and see me."

Hoboes: spirits of the night, lonely figures atop railway cars; going by catchy first names; telling time by the sun and moon.

We wanted to travel the tracks with hoboes, and so we bought cigarettes at a store in McGehee, Arkansas. Cigarettes would be our letters of introduction. We walked over to the railroad yard. Packs of Philip Morrisses and Winstons bulged from our shirt pockets, pants pockets.

A big guy came out of the Union Pacific Railroad office, dressed scrubbily.

"Who the hell y'all think y'all are, somethin' out of Mark Twain? I'll be goddamn." He laughed at us and yet tried to be

Lite
BEER

genial. The Arkansas accent was thick as syrup. We asked about hoboes. "Hell, yeah, stick around today, you'll see some hoboes," Gerald Birchfield said. He spit a wad of tobacco juice two feet into the air and it looked like someone had tossed a handful of pennies.

"Damn hobo came through here last summer, name Mountain Dew. He hopped off the train right here in this yard. Had a sack of money with him. The next day he left town driving a Cadillac. Figure that out, 'cause I sure can't." Another wad of juice flew.

Once, late at night, he said, he walked deep into the yard to check some tracks. He was stopped by a whisper. When he looked around, finally zeroing in on the whisper, he noticed a hobo, crouched like a baseball catcher, who said, "Hey, bud, you got a cigarette?"

Thirty cars must have come and gone through the railroad yard. We looked between them and on top of them. No hoboes. By evening we were heading on. Just outside McGehee there was a gaunt man on thin legs headed up the road.

"Howdy, Byron Schutt, just out here traveling the country. Left Santa Fe couple weeks ago. Was in a bar one night there and four women surrounded me. I think they wanted to get me in bed. I got out of there fast as I could. The world's all shot to hell now. Course you must know that."

"Are you a hobo?"

"*Weeellll*," he said, his eyes getting wide, "I wouldn't go that far." He paused as if to ponder his station in life. "You ever hear that line from that Merle Haggard song — 'I'm a common man and my dog's got no pedigree'? That's me." When we asked him if he wanted a lift, he said, "Nope," and walked on, down a lonesome road.

Less than seven hundred people lived in Arkansas City, Arkansas. Stan let me out on one corner, to do a little walking. He rode up on the levee to look at the river. We'd meet up.

I turned a corner in the quiet of day, and a pretty green lawn gave way to the Desha County Courthouse, which rose like an old Greek revival structure. Flowers grew on both sides of the courthouse steps.

A woman sat in her car in front of the courthouse. The front door was flung open to the sun but she sat back under the roof, which shaded her from the sun.

"Got problems with the house," Bertha McGowan said, looking at the courthouse, as if addressing it and not me.

Walter Powell, Helena, Arkansas

She had saved most of her life to be able to make mortgage payments on her home. The other day a letter had come in the mail about some kind of tax problem with her home. Three weeks ago she was ill, was just now recovering. But when the letter came she got out of bed and got in her old, dependable two-door Falcon and drove nonstop to the courthouse. "My grandson said I'd never drive again. Ha."

A man walked out of the courthouse. She recognized him and said hello, but he did not respond. "He's deaf as I am," she said. "He used to have to carry his wife to the hospital every night. She passed away. He don't have no one left now but a daughter. He don't do much anymore but fish."

There was a one-room jail house next to the courthouse and now her eyes were resting on the jail house. "Some man snatched a woman's pocketbook the other day. He was over here in jail before he knew it."

Her gray-and-black hair was done up in a nice bun, and the strap of a patent-leather purse lay around her small wrist.

She had gone to college to be a schoolteacher. "That's what country folks do, teach. I taught seventh and eighth grades." She lived alone now. Her only daughter lived out of state.

"Me and my husband separated," she said in a soft and direct voice. "I asked for my name back and they gave it to me. I wear my daddy's name." A little kick in the voice came with the latter part of the statement.

I asked her if she wanted me to escort her up to the courthouse.

"No, don't put yourself through any trouble. I can make it on my own."

"No trouble. I'm going inside to take a look around anyway." I began to feel like a surrogate son.

"Well, if you're going up there, I might as well go with you."

She leaned on my arm and we walked up the steps to the courthouse. A woman behind a desk raised her head and greeted Bertha McGowan. "Why, hello, Mrs. McGowan. What brings you here?" McGowan walked into an office, stayed for a few minutes, then came out. The tax official whom Bertha McGowan would have to see was not in. "Guess I'll have to come back Monday," she said.

"How about something cold to drink?"

"No. No need to trouble yourself."

"It's no trouble."

"Well," she said, taking a seat in the sun-splashed hallway, "maybe one of them little bitty colas."

I shoved two quarters into the soda machine, one for her and one for myself.

Willie Henderson

"My husband still lives in town," she said. She began to look around, as if he'd pop out from some corner.

"When you finish your trip," she said, "write me a letter sometime."

I made my way to the door. Her hand was still wrapped around the neck of the little bitty cola. She smiled and the smile came across the bar of light coming through the tall windows. At the last moment, before I left, she turned her eyes away quickly, like a shy woman.

I went and looked for Stan, circling one side of the town and passing the liquor store and post office. Then I turned toward another side of town and spotted him sitting under an oak tree in a swing tied to the tree by rope. An old man sat next to him and another man sat a few feet away.

The old man was Willie Henderson, and his friend in the wheelchair was Bernard Hampton. Age set 112-year-old Willie Henderson in the shade; war wounds set his friend in the wheelchair. A black cane rested between Willie Henderson's legs and an old gnarled hand was fixed around the head of the cane.

Willie Henderson was born in Rolling Fork, Mississippi, and raised on a plantation. His mother and father were born slaves. He went to school on the plantation, a one-room schoolhouse, but it was just for a short while. "I was expelled from school in the first grade 'cause I was out in the yard and kept looking at this yellow girl."

A little less than a century ago he came to Arkansas to work on the Mississippi River as a logger. "I worked and stayed in the logging camps up and down the river. I put all my money on clothes and the woman I had," he said. His long-collared shirt was buttoned to the neck. His shoes were dusty with the dust of Arkansas. There were cataracts in his eyes, so they looked at us and went past us, but we did not notice too much that the eyeballs strayed.

His wife had died five years ago. Some days he'd get up and start walking along these roads, not seeing his way clearly because of the cataracts, and wind up at the foot of his wife's grave in the cemetery. "I never had my wife cook for nobody but me," he said, and this was a point of pride.

"He don't got nobody now," the friend Bernard Hampton said. "I'm about the only one around here he's got."

At Willie Henderson's side was a sack with a bottle in it. Every now and then he'd take a swallow of Old Crow, lifting it to his lips with unsteady hands. "It keeps him alive," Hampton said.

Last winter, during a period when there was hail in the wind and the temperature dropped below thirty degrees, no one saw

Henderson for several days. At first no one worried, but as the days passed the worry began. Some neighbors went to check on him. They banged on the door and there was no answer, so they had to break it down. Henderson was lying there, frozen, "stiff as a board," said Hampton. His arms were folded across his chest, as if in eternal contentment.

At the hospital, friends paced the halls. But the doctor said Willie was lucky, that he'd been found in time and would pull through. He was home in a week.

"Say you from Boston? Never been there," Willie said. "That's where the ocean's at. It's cold up there." He laughed, switched the cane to the other hand, crossed his legs. There was something about the dust on his shoes and the gnarled hands and the good friend Bernard Hampton that made Willie Henderson seem righteous as rain.

Stan shifted the gears from park to drive and Willie Henderson raised his bottle of Old Crow to the air, to us, and we cruised from the shade onto the bright road.

The Mississippi road opened beautifully onto green fields edged in rich black dirt. Birds flew out in front of the car and the air was clear and sweet, with swing music in it. Then one of the birds got too close and crashed into the windshield, and that took some of the music from the air.

A breakfast of grits and eggs and bacon was had at a roadside restaurant in Mayersville, Mississippi, and after breakfast, as we rode through the town, children watched our slow-moving car as if we were ushering in a parade. Grown folks sat on porches fanning themselves. The heat socked us as if it were a fist. The road turned and a man sat in a pickup, looking at his fingernails.

Ask a man how his life is going and he may pass on the question. He may also answer: "Time is at hand. Things predicted by God will come true. This place is nothing, and yet is the essence of everything."

His name was Robert McGee. He was given to the mystical, yet there were woes in his daily life. He was a preacher without a church, a worker without a job.

"I was over in Arkansas, working. I asked the boss if I could deliver a sermon. He told me I had to do it on my own time." This upset McGee. One day he left work early. "I had to come home because I felt one of my daughters needed me."

When he returned to work he found he did not have a job. The boss told him he was laid off, and McGee thought it had to do with his desire to preach on the job.

Willie Henderson

He went down to the unemployment office and explained everything, about the religion and all, but the checks had not started to come. He went inside his house and brought back a piece of pink paper that the unemployment office had given him. "They're still reviewing the case," he said, perplexed. The breeze blew the edges of the paper and he folded it carefully, an important document, and put it in his shirt pocket.

He was married, and his wife found no consolation in his urge to preach. She did not condemn it; just talked pragmatically of their two little children, of mouths to feed. Between the choice of gospel for the soul and food for the children, she sided with food for the children.

"My wife, she don't understand," McGee said.

He had dark, smooth skin, and looked like the great actor Sidney Poitier must have looked when he was in his thirties.

No church in Mayersville would let McGee climb its pulpit. They told him he was inexperienced. He was resigned to that and said he might eventually have to put the Bibles in the back of the pickup and just hit the road, "to spread the word," is how he put it. He longed to tell about the troubles in the river cities.

He looked out onto the pretty Mississippi land. Morning floated along. Parts of dandelions, broken by wind, incremental orphans of nature now, floated above the high grass, where they dipped and rose and dipped again. Where others saw the beauty of the land, McGee saw land that was but a Bible flung open, where grass grew from the pages.

"Where is the river?" I asked.

"Yonder, over the hill," he pointed, and I asked if he wanted to ride up to it.

"Sure."

At the top of the hill I slowed the car to a crawl and noticed the river, just beyond the trees. It gleamed like a plate of good china turned upward to the sun. I parked the car under the shade of a tall tree. He pointed out a grain elevator, the main source of employment in town, a half mile downriver.

Then his voice lowered a note. He explained that he had been in a car wreck last year. He'd been behind the wheel. A little boy had died. There was a scar on his forehead, not noticeable twenty minutes ago, now, given the circumstances, almost dramatic.

"Why did the Lord spare *me*? You see what I'm saying? Why did the Lord spare *me*? It had to be so I could spread the word. I got to tell the people that time is of the essence."

He paused, looked out across the river, then back at me and said, "God is not through with me yet. And in due time I'm praying that my wife will understand."

Vicksburg, Mississippi

In the early afternoon we all gathered and sat in the front yard of Otis Parker's house. He was McGee's next-door neighbor.

Parker sat smoking a pipe. He rubbed a pained knee with his hands. "Hurt it sixty years ago playing baseball. I was running for this fly ball. Never saw the tree." The knee was busted, and since his family was unable to afford surgery, it healed on its own, crudely.

Otis Parker also was a religious man. When he started talking to McGee, the conversation took on an almost mystical quality.

"The Lord's coming, yes He is," said Parker.

"Anytime now," said McGee, "anytime now."

"Oh, He could come at midnight. You can't fool Him," Parker offered.

Before McGee could follow, his wife came to the screen door, like an apparition, and without words passing between them, he bade everyone farewell and went up the steps into his house.

More than 80 percent of the population of Mayersville was black. With numbers and the right to vote came political clout. The mayor was a black woman, Unita Blackwell. Her green-roofed house was on a stretch of land in the northeast corner of town.

"I'll talk as soon as I'm finished on the phone. Y'all want something, just go in the kitchen and get it. This is the South."

We went into the kitchen to get water. A few minutes later she noticed our glasses, still nearly full: after the water had settled, we had noticed particles in the brown-tinted water. "We just got a new sewer system. Still trying to work some of the kinks out."

She flopped down in an armchair, under the ceiling fan.

She was a big, expressive woman who got her political start in the sixties, working with the Student Non-violent Coordinating Committee. She was the first black woman to be elected mayor in the state of Mississippi.

"Held my first city hall meeting right here in this living room," she said. "This *was* city hall."

Still, no dramatic economic changes had taken place there. It was mostly poor folks and old homes.

"But lots has changed here," she said. "Twenty years ago, black and white like you couldn't have come in this town without causing a whole lot of trouble."

The social change may have been sweet, but the economic outlook was bitter. "Well, we need some money to do things."

"I am trying to get the farmers to cooperate with a plan for the river," she said, envisioning a lively riverfront, stores, shops. She also had plans for a nursery and a recreation center, "to keep the young ones out of trouble."

"Years ago — and *way* before my time," she stressed, "there was a hotel, eight saloons, and a Chinese laundry."

Otis Parker, Mayersville, Mississippi

Now there was just the post office and the restaurant at the end of town and two mom-and-pop stores fighting it out for survival.

If she gets a chance to put her blueprint into action, she promised that "the river will roll again."

Fast-food outlets lined the four-lane leading into Greenville, Mississippi. A line at a Dairy Queen stretched ten back. We passed it up. In the sixties this was a hot southern town, racial strife tearing at its seams. The newspaper, the *Greenville Delta-Democrat,* editorialized for racial harmony, civil rights, equality. It rubbed many whites the wrong way. Rednecks threatened the paper's publisher, a big man named Hodding Carter, Sr. His life was threatened often enough that he was forced to pack a pistol. Warily, he'd walk to his car in the Mississippi night, listening for odd noises, watching the shadows. Now Carter's gone and the newspaper's been bought. Of course his son, Hodding Carter, Jr., went up to Washington, D.C., a few years back to work for President Jimmy Carter.

Down at the levee two women fished. A few yards in front of them, on a docked boat, a sign hung in clear view: NO FISHING. Stan took a picture. One of the women turned and yelled, "Don't go taking my picture! I bet you from the newspaper. Get outta here." She raised her pole from the water, and I thought she would fling it at us, but she didn't.

From the levee we saw boats race in the water, jumping over the waves. Girls sat atop the levee in souped-up cars, probably the cars of their boyfriends, out racing and jumping over the waves.

It was secession, states dropping from the Union and forming their own renegade governments. South Carolina and North Carolina. Georgia. Alabama. Mississippi. A handful of other southern states, all revolting against pressure to end slavery and for states' rights. The insurrection flowed into war, the Civil War.

The South needed a leader for their cause. On February 10, 1861, at a meeting of the new government, Kentucky-born Jefferson Davis was chosen to preside over the Confederacy.

He was a West Pointer with an undistinguished academy record, said to be a gentleman, known to be temperamental, a lover of Milton and Shakespeare. Called to duty, he went, filled with the air of southern aristocracy, tradition, and manners. "All we ask is to be left alone," he said.

Robert E. Lee, always outmanned, was the most renowned of the Confederate generals. Some have said he thought the war a dubious enterprise from the beginning. But he was a southerner, son of a prominent Virginia family, and so he went, rising in the smoke of battle. He was past fifty when he led the Confederates, and day by day, his body grew more racked from the brutalities of war. There was no way he could turn the clock back, make himself young, so he had to fight the war as a fifty-year-old man might, by spirit, mind over matter, and strategy. There was something cool, almost aristocratic, about him. The South was falling at his feet, but he soldiered on, the victories few and far between. His men were hungry, ill-clothed, and confused, and they were dying. He soldiered on into the night, the rebel yell sounding glorious, coursing through the veins now like blood.

A year before he joined up with the North, Ulysses S. Grant was working in a general store and collecting back rents for his family. He was moody, hard to figure, not talkative, nearly an outcast. His record at West Point had been average, but he had performed beautifully in the Mexican War. Away from war he was like a great athlete barred from competing. He needed war, he needed that thing that is Olympian in its savagery. Time would show him to be a son of war.

"I have known a few men who were always aching for a fight when there was no enemy near, who were as good as their word when the battle did come," Ulysses S. Grant once said.

And he would rise again in the Civil War, riding in navy blue, gold bars on his shoulders. He didn't sit under tents all night studying maps. He just went. He could almost sit up on his horse and sniff where the enemy was. Then he just pointed and his men went, bulling onward.

"Find out where your enemy is. Get at him as soon as you can. Strike at him as hard as you can and as often as you can, and keep moving on." That was his motto.

He rode atop his horse, fearless, weaponless, through forests, along riverbanks, unshaven, unkempt.

F. Scott Fitzgerald once compared one of his characters to Grant: "The hero, like Grant, lolling in his general store in Galena, is ready to be called to an intricate destiny."

Some questioned his style, his tactics, said he was wild, just a buccaneer and not a true soldier. He laughed and said look at the dead Confederate bodies, count them, tally up.

An officer once approached Lincoln and urged him to demote Grant. "No," Lincoln replied. "I cannot spare the man. He fights."

The war would rage for four years. About four hundred men dropped to the ground each day. General William Tecumseh

Vicksburg, Mississippi

Sherman, late in the campaign, blew into Atlanta, kicked it in, then burned it to the ground. In the spring of 1865 the end was near. Lee surrendered at Appomattox.

Davis, encamped at the Confederate capital of Richmond, broke into the night on April 2, 1865, a band of his followers with him. They figured to start the war anew, from Texas.

Lincoln showed up at Richmond and ordered troops after Davis, who was caught beside a campfire on May 10 near Texas. At first it was thought Davis would be hanged for leading an insurrection, but after months in prison, favorable sentiment, not only from the South, but from the North as well, grew. He was released.

(It took a southern-born president, Jimmy Carter, to sign a resolution, on October 17, 1978, that gave Jefferson Davis his citizenship back, restoring some of the glory that must have been inside his heart when he took off on his mission.)

What became of Lee? Of Grant?

Robert E. Lee went on to become a college president. On the day he died he had said, "Strike the tent."

Grant went on to become a two-term president of the United States, his administration racked by ineptness, corruption, his cabinet members constantly being investigated. To him, criticism was merely complaints from the enemy. But in the White House he seemed misplaced, an interloper, an unsophisticated man ignorant of a politician's craft, unsmooth and unable to realize that the nation was more than a band of soldiers.

He left office with whispers over his shoulders, the whiff of scandal everywhere. He went abroad, traveled the world like a highly respected travel writer. Abroad, they hadn't realized his political miscalculations. They knew only of the great war victories. Once, in England, a crowd of nearly eighty thousand saluted him. An old general.

To stave off debt late in life, he struggled on his deathbed and wrote his memoirs. They are noted for their plainness and beautiful simplicity. A man name Samuel Clemens published them.

The fields in Vicksburg, Mississippi, were green, and the valleys of the Vicksburg National Cemetery stretched into the distance and rolled off toward the river. It was easy to imagine, on this somnolent afternoon, soldiers coming up over the hills and cannons being fired and gunboats coming down the Mississippi River.

After the battle of Vicksburg, Jefferson Davis wrote to Lieutenant General John Pemberton, commander at Vicksburg: "I

thought and still think you did right to risk an army for the purpose of keeping command of even a section of the Mississippi River. Had you succeeded, none would have blamed, had you not made the attempt, few would have defended your course."

Stones marking the Civil War dead in this cemetery leaned to the river, and the aura of war lingered and seemed to carry across the river like the wispy pieces of cotton that floated over it in the late evening.

For decades after the war, blacks left the South in massive numbers to settle in northern cities, looking for economic chances. But time changed things, and blacks began returning to the South in the early 1970s in large numbers. The land that was never their land, but in a way would always be their land, pulled. They were always foreigners in Brooklyn, New York, anyway, so they returned to the South, to whatever it was that made their father's father and mother's mother endure. They came back to things left behind.

Arlean Williams, born here in Vicksburg, had just returned after twenty years of living in Brooklyn. Her house, on a rising hill above a valley, sat on stilts, a shout from the river.

There was a garden of okra, collard greens, and lima beans that she stood in front of in the backyard. The cats, she said, had been going into the garden and eating the vegetables before she could get them to the dinner table.

Underneath the raised house it was dark and several of the cats moved about in the shadows. They licked water that dripped from a long pipe onto the rocks. Their eyes shone like green and yellow marbles.

"I might have to put a fence up," she said, and turned and looked under the house at the indicted cats. Then she raised back up and squared off with the clear air. A rooster crowed.

Above: Confederate Cemetery, Helena, Arkansas Left: National Cemetery, Vicksburg, Mississippi

Beyond the garden, the land dropped and railroad tracks were at the bottom of the valley. A hill with kudzu vines draping it rose away from the railroad tracks. When Arlean Williams fell asleep here on that first night back from Brooklyn, the train rumbled by on the railroad tracks. "Goodness, I jumped clean out of bed, I didn't know what that was." Now she was used to the rumbling.

Her old house needed repairs. "I just wanted to come back to the land. I'm thinking of having my own home built. That would be nice, real nice."

Summertime in Natchez, Mississippi, and we were down at the dock, eating catfish skinned beautifully boneless by one Steve Stephens. He and his wife, Rita, waved us down, just said, "Come on down here" as if we were cousins or something. There was red beans and rice to go with the catfish.

"You want something to drink, look in the cooler," Rita said.

Southern hospitality, seventy-five in the shade; the catfish kept on jumping. There were a few others at the table: a couple of fishermen, a guy named Chuck, and his girl, Laura, both up from New Orleans.

Steve kept plopping catfish in a fryer and unloading them onto the plates from a cardboard box. He worked for the oil companies, checking the wells along the river. His wife ran the dock.

Talk was layered with stories about the river, which was just under everyone's feet, at the corner of our eyes.

Once, they were having dinner, right on this dock, and a body floated by, its belly up, white as cotton, a drowned man. Steve reached for his big hook on the wall and pulled the body from the river. The police found the man's suicide note a day later.

There was that March day in 1980 when Steve and Rita were down here and the rain just kept coming and coming, all morning long, rain and more rain. Steve began to feel an itch, the kind of itch that maybe only someone who had been on the river forty years could feel. He looked up from the dock at the commercial strip and told Rita he didn't feel comfortable, said he thought the rain might cause a mudslide, and he started to walk up the hill to tell the shopkeepers to lock up and go home.

"Don't go frightening those people," Rita had said. Then it happened.

"I looked up," she recalled, "and there were six cars over the bluff." The roofs of shops caved in, screams were heard in the air. Steve turned away from the hill and started for his wife at the dock instead, figuring the mud was headed down to her. He

Natchez, Mississippi

screamed, telling her to jump in the river, but she couldn't move. Fright.

"And then it was as if God had put his hand up and just said *Stop!*" Rita said. Steve and some rescue workers pulled two dead bodies from the wreckage.

There was talk about their only son, Mike, who ran away from home when he was sixteen. Like Huck Finn, Mike had just lit out for the territory ahead of him. He hitchhiked around and found a job on the tugboats going up and down the river. He'd call home every now and then to let his mom know what state he was in. Mike was twenty-seven now, back home, married, with a wife and two daughters.

Later, after we had eaten all the catfish we could eat, and after the sun had slid off the surface of the river, Chuck and Laura, who had been sitting at the dock, asked if we wanted to go out with them in their boat, to watch the sun set.

Chuck Evans was a contractor from New Orleans, said he had come up to Natchez to ride his boat "because the river's prettier up here."

It was wonderful to be back out there on the river, to feel the water bounce up from the surface and touch the skin, to feel the wet coolness at the neck.

Chuck guided the boat into a back region of the Old River and turned off the engine, letting the boat drift. Thin rust-colored tree trunks rose from the water and reflected on the surface. The leaves of trees hung like giant curtains. Water lilies floated by, insects riding on top. The sun glowed orange and the silence was true.

Stan snapped pictures. I leaned back. Laura murmured about the loveliness of the river back here. Chuck stood. On a seven-second count, the sun dropped.

And then, one by one, it seemed, we noticed it was dark, dark everywhere, climbing dark, and we all looked around, as if awakened from a stupor. Chuck eased the boat backward through the trees that now blended with the dark.

"We have to figure out how to get out of here," Chuck said.

And Stan said, "We can't stay out here all night. The mosquitoes will kill us." They had begun to attack.

Stan and I had been in similar situations before, on the raft, afloat in darkness. We reached for the oars, measured the water, knowing to keep the boat from the shallows, and used the oars to push away from the trees that the front of the boat slammed as we drifted backward. We felt for live logs (movable) and dead logs (immovable). It grew chilly. We saw a flicker of light, then a long beam of light, and Chuck said it was light from shore and guided the boat toward it.

Natchez, Mississippi

Under-the-Hill, Natchez

Vidalia, Louisiana

"*Stop!*" Stan and I yelled. We knew it was not light from shore but the light of a barge. A minute later the barge roared by, its black body melted into the river. Hearts skipped beats.

We drifted on and finally spotted lights from shore. Forty minutes later, as we pulled into the dock, the Natchez fire chief and some of his men were on the dock. The chief, a small man with a tough face, stood flat-footed.

"Y'all are very lucky. Only one in five boaters ever makes it back from that area out there after dark — and I'm talking professional boaters."

Laura said she needed a drink.

That night we sat on the porch of the home where we rented rooms, talked with Chuck and Laura, looked out at the river, and admired the way it rolled. We were glad to be alive. There was freshly baked gingerbread to eat, and the air around us smelled like gingerbread.

At five the next morning, Steve and Rita's son, Mike Stephens, met us at the dock so we could accompany him and his father on their inspection of the oil wells they managed.

"Damn, it's cold out here," Mike said, getting out of his car. We stood in the cold like children, shivering, sleepy.

We would have to ride over to the Louisiana side of the river to meet Steve. Mike pulled out a cigarette and lit a match, resting it in his cupped palm. His face glowed orange in the still darkness. He blew the match, tossed it in the river, guided the boat out of the dock. It bounced and bounced, and specks of water tapped us in the face. Daylight started being squeezed into the sky as if from a tube of toothpaste, and the boat just bounced along in the cold.

Armadillo, Angola, Louisiana

We tied the boat to a tree deep inside a bend. "My dad should be here any minute," Mike said.

We waited on land. Mike pulled out another cigarette. There was the thinnest film of dark oil under his fingernails; I had noticed the same dark layer under the nails of his father the day before. In the son there were echoes of the father.

He told about his marriage. He first met his wife in high school but didn't marry her until years later, when he was back from wandering.

"I liked to black out at the wedding rehearsal," he said. He had had to turn to some friends and say, "Get me out of here." Outside, in the air, he got his courage back, and later went through with the rehearsal.

He admitted he liked married life; liked to do a lot of the cooking. "Taught my wife a few things about cooking even."

He looked out onto the river. A friend who drowned came to mind. "His little boy had walked out there on a sandbar. So my friend, his daddy, takes off running. He never reached him; slipped off to the side of the sandbar. Came up once, his wife said, and didn't come up again. My dad fished him out of the river. The little boy never fell in. Heck, it happened right back there in the part of the river y'all was lost in last night."

The father drove up, shifted gears on a four-wheel-drive pickup. "Morning," he said.

"Morning."

Stan hopped into the front. Mike and I took the back of the truck.

Mike was rail thin.

"Heard you ran away from home," I said.

He grinned, but just a little. "Yep, wasn't getting along with my old man."

He said he walked roads, bummed rides, slept under bridges. "I wouldn't do it now. Bunch of crazy sons of bitches out there."

He had no complaints about any of it. And things brightened a lot when he got his job riding barges up and down the Mississippi and Ohio rivers. Once, on the Ohio, near Cincinnati, he walked out to the edge of a barge to check some rope. It was raining. When he pulled on the rope he slipped and fell overboard.

"I'd of drowned if one of the fellas on board hadn't of seen me fall," he said.

Vidalia, Louisiana

Steve brought the truck to a stop on a wide layer of rich, dark mud. Cracks spread across the mud, as if it had been baked, but it was as soft as putty. Oil wells were pumping furiously; the morning sun gleamed down on them. The wells dug about two thousand feet under the river, Steve said.

"This here has been a mighty good little field. This particular well has made millions." But the money, he said, was split between investors and leasers and even geologists. He said this divvying up of the money took some of the glamour away. It was no longer like it was when he came over from Morgan City back in 1951, "A wildcatter's dream back then," he said. Steve had had a job in those days ferrying oil crews across the river.

"It's all such a gamble," he said, about playing the oil wells. He'd seen investors come out to the wells at dawn, stand on the land, and start to sweat as if they were in the desert. The ones who win, even if they lose in a future investment, are hooked. "Can't get it out of their system after they've hit once," he said.

Steve invested once. "I worried too much." He lost too. So now he worked for seven different oil companies, checking the production levels of the wells every morning.

He turned on a spigot and oil oozed out across his hand, green, slick as slime. "This here's oil right out of the river," he said.

It can be a dangerous job. He's seen wells get too hot, ignite, and just blow, flames shooting up, whispering against the air.

"Once an oil well blew, threw a young boy twenty feet in the air. He landed, got up, and ran right into the woods."

Steve had three blue-tipped pens in the shoulder pocket of his jumpsuit, and a gold-plated pocket watch in his pocket. "It's ten-thirty. Let's go check some other wells."

The truck bounced and struggled through mud. Branches from trees slapped at the sides of the truck because the road was so narrow.

"You hear of Nellie's?" Mike asked, from the back of the truck.

"Nellie's? No, what's that?"

"A whorehouse. You ain't heard of Nellie's? It's a legal whorehouse."

"In Natchez?"

"Yep, I'll have to show it to you before you leave."

I quickly scrawled a message down in my notebook: Go to Nellie's.

We checked in on a few other wells, then Steve parked the truck and we walked deep into the woods to check traps he'd set for crawfish. He approached a muddy stream of backwater, walked right in, as if there were no water there, lifted the trap, and the little crawfish started squirming, clawing to get out.

He checked another trap and pulled a big catfish from it, at least ten pounds. "Good eating," Steve said. "Damn good eating."

As we walked back to the truck, Steve swiped brush away with bare hands. He did it with such ease he could have been walking across a ballroom. His walk was direct, uninterrupted. Everyone else hustled to keep up with him.

"The older I get," he said, "I notice there are more and more

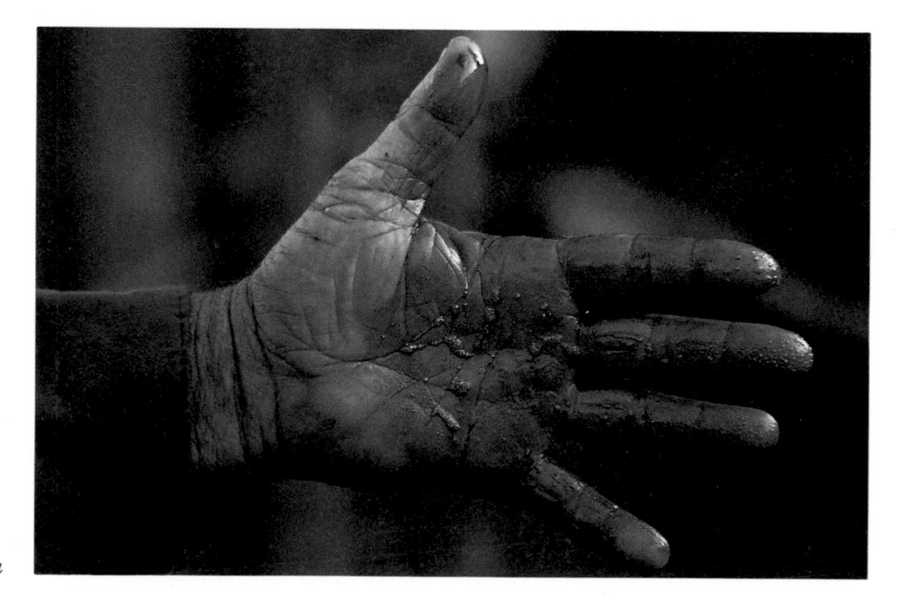

Oil, Vidalia, Louisiana

times when I'm back here, walking, and I'll start to feel a little tired. So I'll just stop and take a little nap."

After lunch Mike took us over to Nellie's. Turned out the whorehouse was a remnant from the old riverboat days. No one had ever had the desire to shut it down. It always had been business as usual.

A ten-foot-high fence stretched around the house, on Rankin Street. There was a white Lincoln Continental in the driveway. I knocked. Stan and Mike stood to the side. A woman came, opened the door so there was just the screen door between her and me. She was wearing red, see-through.

"What y'all want?"

Her face was attractive, but her body was a little overweight. She seemed to realize the face was the key. The smile still had some charm in it.

"Is Nellie home? I'd like to talk to her."

"Nellie's asleep," she said, opening the door, letting us in. It was dark. We were in the kitchen. The door that led from the kitchen to the other part of the large house was closed. I strained to hear sounds of illicit activity, but no sounds came from behind the closed door.

She reached atop the refrigerator and pulled down a box. She pulled the top from the box and brought out a handful of T-shirts. She unfolded one of the T-shirts and stood before us like a salesclerk. The T-shirt said NELLIE'S PLACE. NATCHEZ, MISSISSIPPI.

"Y'all want to buy a T-shirt?" She seemed very sincere.

"No."

"No."

"Nope."

We had spoken.

She put the T-shirts away. "Well, I ain't got time to stand here talking. I got to get ready for church." She was already at the screen door, holding it open for us.

In the morning, when we woke and walked out to the porch and looked to our left, we saw two big steamboats anchored in the river, as if they had come to pick us up. We talked our way onto one of them, the *Mississippi Queen*. It was to leave in one hour. We went and quickly packed, said bye to Chuck and Laura, but couldn't find Steve and Rita. We drove to the river, locked up the car, and walked down the hill to the boat. I was grinning, as if I had gold coins in my pockets. A skinny kid came down to the landing to help us load up.

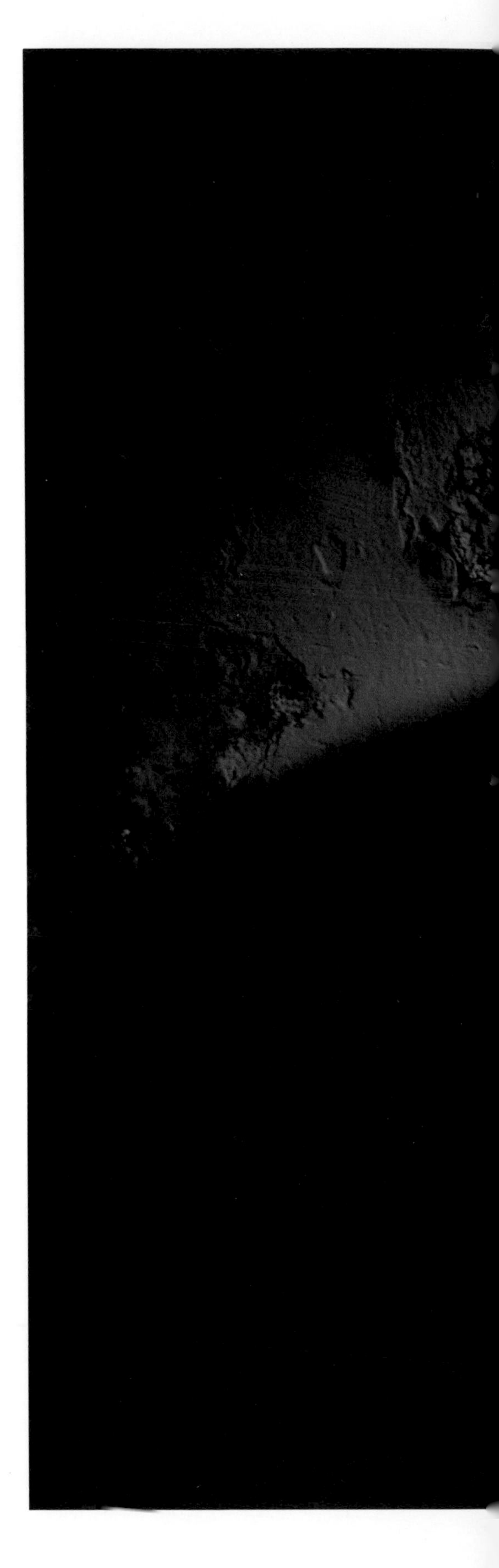

Natchez, Mississippi

This was Mike Suadi's first summer working on the boat. He was a busboy. The first day he started work, he explained, as he walked along the deck, he stepped into the kitchen, dishes stacked high in both arms, and slipped on a pool of grease: Jerry Lewis. "Man, the dishes went just everywhere. I mean everywhere. But I managed to keep my balance. I got rhythm."

He led us down a hallway on the lower deck, and we unpacked in a very small room.

Mike said he liked the job, and now even understood why so many of the passengers were older than he. "Hey, these people grew up with Mark Twain. I can understand that."

The big red paddlewheel in the back of the boat pushed water around and around as the boat eased from the landing. There was music from the calliope. The captain of the boat was on the upper deck, dressed in starched white, waving to the people of Vicksburg below.

"It's kind of sad when you leave a town," Captain Harold DeMarrero said, the sound of the boat's whistle in the soft Mississippi air.

Couples leaned over the deck railings and waved at the people on the banks.

"This is the only romance left on the river," the captain said.

Harold DeMarrero was a fifth-generation steamboat captain. Among the items that were in his cabin, two stood out: the bottle of Pierre Jouet champagne, and the framed picture of Mark Twain, with this quote underneath: "It were not best that we should all think alike; it is difference of opinion that makes horse races."

The boat drifted, above the land, parallel with rooftops, bluffs, treetops. Small boats cleared away, cutting nearly over to the opposite edge of the river to avoid the steamboat.

Shirtless men played shuffleboard on the top deck; their wives sat nearby. Sometimes a wife rose and pushed a disc down the way, then laughed it off, and the laughter drifted overboard. The day wore on, gently, serenely. A kid tied a kite to the railing and the kite sailed among the clouds. The boat moved into sunset, then evening.

Evening on a steamboat, and now the crew was all slicked up, dressed in formal attire. The dining room buzzed and fresh flowers were everywhere, as if to affirm the beautiful lightness of it all. Waiters and waitresses moved about coolly and carefully. The gleam of silverware — knives, forks, spoons — was everywhere. The touching of it caused distant tingling.

A woman in a blue dress sat at the Baldwin piano and tapped tunes softly. Sounded like Gershwin; could have been Porter. Pearls (of course) hung from her thin neck. Every now and then

Delta Queen, ***New Orleans***

Mississippi Queen

her lips moved, for she had broken into song, but very mildly, and one could not tell if she was singing to herself, a sort of pantomime, or to the passengers seated nearest to her. It mattered little.

Passengers were dressed elegantly. The chandeliers meshed with the china, which meshed with the silverware, which meshed with the earrings that hung from the ears of the women. A riot of things rich, smooth, and right.

Linen napkins fell across laps; reflections bounced from mirrors. Couples leaned into each other, whispered, coming close enough to kiss, then pulled back to whisper some more, their voices light.

We ordered trout, asparagus, ale with a twist of lime.

Outside the window it was dark. The moon looked as if one of the well-heeled passengers had pulled a coin from his pocket and flicked it over his shoulder, rolling it into the sky. A silver-dollar moon.

After dinner there was jazz by the Phil Gomez Band, Dixieland, and the couples who had been eating were now dancing, and it seemed that the champagne they drank was gliding them across the dance floor.

We strolled to the upper deck, sat under the sky in lawn chairs, watched the dark move. Stan dozed off. I got up and walked around the decks. Couples passed.

She stepped out of a hallway into the shadows of the lower deck. We had exchanged glances earlier. Her eyes were kind and big, and there was a richness and sureness about her. We spoke; her voice was distinctive, almost a soft kind of hoarseness. We walked to the railing, watched the mist rise up from the river, listened to the boat go deeper into the night, and talked more softly, so as not to disturb the stars.

Four years ago Bobby Sherman walked down to the *Mississippi Queen* steamboat, anchored in Cincinnati at the time, and asked about a summer job. "I figured I'd save up a little money for law school," he said.

He started out as a deckhand. "Then I met a girl." Even though the girl was gone now, he'd been riding the river ever since. He was the chief maître d'. He also watched over the crew, soothed problems.

One time a guy and a girl on the boat got into an argument, he said. The guy jumped overboard. Maybe it was a suicide attempt over love gone awry. "We found him three hours later, downriver, floating on a log," Bobby said. They threw the guy a rope and pulled him in. He was let off at the next town. A member of the crew had suggested counseling.

Once, a crew member, a guy known as Big Daddy, got up on one of the tables at a crew party and started singing "Rainy Night in Georgia." By the time he was finished with the song he had stripped buck naked.

Then Bobby told a story with a ring of derring-do: one night, ten miles from New Orleans, he, with a tuxedo folded neatly and tucked inside a plastic bag wrapped around his waist, jumped overboard, started swimming, and vanished in the dark river. A few on board wondered if they'd ever see Bobby again.

When the boat docked in New Orleans, Bobby Sherman was on the landing, dressed in the tux, grinning like a matinee idol. He led the way down Bourbon Street.

By breakfast the boat had anchored smoothly in Vicksburg. A few of the crew members egged Stan and me on about playing basketball. We dashed to the boat's gift shop, bought gym shorts, then walked up a hill, through the heat, to the Vicksburg YMCA.

Tom Murphy, **Mississippi Queen**

The woman behind the desk said we could play in the gym all day, for just three bucks. It was an old gymnasium, with a shiny wood floor and chalk-white backboards. A huge fan hummed in the corner, cooling. I bounced the ball, tossed in some jump shots, looked at the guys from the boat down at the other end. Then we chose sides, five on five. Stan and I lost the first game.

The guy I was checking, a tall waiter, moved nicely on the court. He had blown by me once and dunked the ball, then loped off down court.

The second game was different. I canned jump shots from deep in the corner, from the top of the key. Once, I took the ball and spun and pushed it between my legs and went up for the jump shot, and when I came down watched the ball sail through the net.

Another one of our forwards, a guy from Louisiana, a waiter, moved around the bucket smooth as a ballet dancer, pushing in four- and five-foot shots.

We were up one bucket and needed one more to win. Stan stood out of bounds, ready to inbound the ball to me. Our eyes connected, and I motioned for him to lob the ball to me. He did. I jumped and grabbed it, threw a fake on my man, and shot the game-winning basket.

"No, that doesn't count, we weren't ready," a busboy from the opposition yelled.

"Like hell," Stan said. Another member of our team said, "Game's over."

Judge Clarence Allgood

There were loud words, and we walked off the court, claiming victory. A minute later they conceded. Everyone shook hands, toweled off, and walked back to the Mississippi River.

After a hearty lunch on board, I caught up with Tom Murphy, chief purser of the *Mississippi Queen.* He was sitting in a corner on the second deck, talking with some parents. A group of children played around a table, rolling like coins dropped from the pockets of their parents.

Murphy rose and strolled across the deck to talk. As he was walking over I heard ice clink in the vodka Gibson in his hands. He was dressed in a tropical wool suit. The fit was flawless and the suit probably tailor-made. Cuff links closed the shirtsleeves.

"I used to take the big ships out of New York City to South America," Murphy said. "That was thirty years ago. Been on ships all my life. Never married. Never married nothing but the ships."

He was in retirement a few years back but got a phone call, and suddenly there was a boat to catch again.

Clarence Allgood sat on the third deck in a white lawn chair, a hearing aid in his ear. "First crossed the river on a ferry when I was seventeen," he said.

For years he hoboed. "Couldn't resist it. It was romantic." On a summer day back in the mid-thirties he was dashing across a railroad yard. He slipped, and the train that was coming sliced a portion of one of his legs clean off. He was roaming with two buddies. They picked him up, fed him whiskey to kill some of the pain, and finally got him to a hospital.

The experience changed his life. He enrolled in college at Auburn University, then went to Birmingham Law School, loading up on night classes, and finished in 1942. In 1962 President John F. Kennedy called and told Allgood he was appointing him a district judge.

When the *Mississippi Queen* stopped at the river towns, he didn't even get off, just sat on the deck and watched the others as they scattered up the hills. "I've seen every one of these towns along the river," he said.

Again, night. The steamboat captain guided the boat, parting the river, sending the waves to lap gently against the bank. Again there was dancing in the ballroom. Things on board seemed forever, as if someone has thrown time overboard.

By morning the boat was back in Natchez. We stood on a bank and waved and watched it drift away. The young woman with the kind eyes waved from the railing. She disappeared downriver and around a bend with the boat. I felt like swimming after her.

We walked down to the dock to see if Steve, the oilman, and

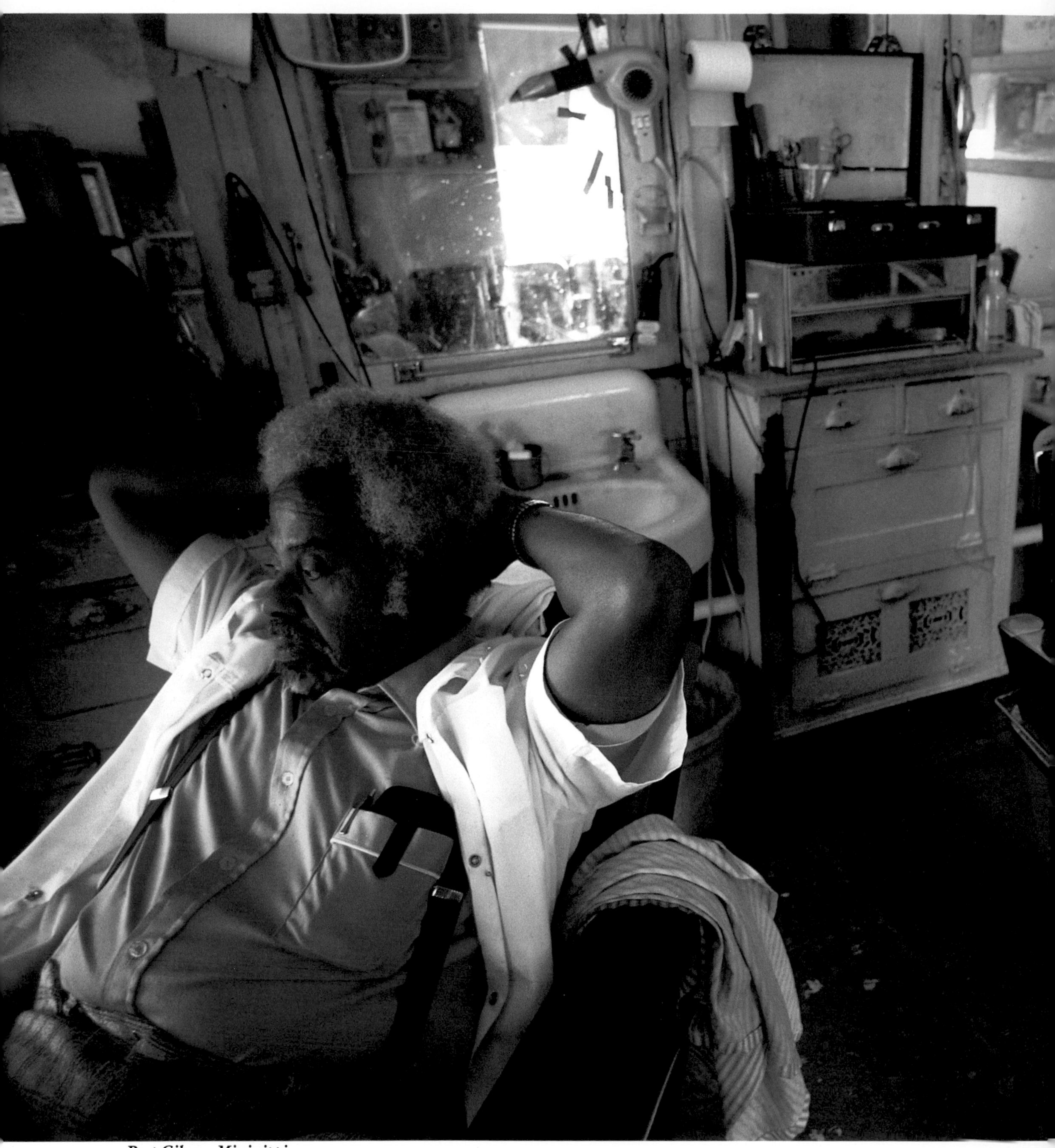

Port Gibson, Mississippi

his wife, Rita, were around. They were not. I scribbled out a little note and left it on a table. I put a rock on top of it so the wind coming off the river would not blow it away.

> *Dear Steve and Rita:*
> *We just returned from the steamboat trip. It was wonderful. We're now heading away again. Thanks for the catfish and the hospitality.*
> *Wil and Stan*

It was the strangest-looking variety store I had ever seen. There were tools on one shelf, and on the shelf under that, loaves of bread, and on another shelf, across the aisle, toys, haphazardly set. The roof leaked, and toward the back, the lights were out and it was dark.

Pete Jordan, the owner, rocked back and forth in a chair. He looked out the window onto the main street of Port Gibson, Mississippi, and said, "This town is dead. They just ain't raised the monument yet." His voice was plain and level. "Cold drinks and cigarettes is about all I sell now."

So far, on this day, there had been three customers. It was nearing six in the evening.

His wife sat in a corner, debating a chicken recipe with another woman.

"What happened here?" I asked.

Jordan, still rocking, said, "Colored boycotted the businesses back in the sixties. Stopped coming into town, wouldn't buy."

The boycott was waged because of unfair hiring practices. "Fifteen of the stores eventually closed," he said. "Never recovered."

The town merchants had sued the boycotters, and won a million-plus settlement from the Mississippi Supreme Court. That scared the hell out of the NAACP, which said such an award would break its back. But the U.S. Supreme Court would overturn the decision.

Stan purchased a ballpoint pen, moving the store's economy just a touch, and we rolled on.

We spent a night in Baton Rouge, circling roads, going down unfamiliar streets. We sat on the grass of the levee and let dark crawl up around us. A guy and his girl sent romantic whoops out across the river.

The next morning a bridge swept us into Delta, Louisiana, and we sat awhile on a porch with Emmanuel Allen.

"I started building this home back in August 1971, with my

Emmanuel Allen, Delta, Louisiana

own hands," he said. "Not quite finished yet, but I got it where I can live in it."

There were pecan trees in the front yard, a cotton field that yawned into the distance, across the road.

Emmanuel Allen had on a shirt and tie. He was retired. There was something charming about a man who got up in the morning and put on shirt and tie to face the day, when the day offered him no desk to sit at.

Last job he had he drove building equipment. He lived alone now. Occasionally the name *Mamie* drifted into his conversation. She was his wife.

"She came home from work one day. It was about two in the afternoon. She went inside and lay down on the couch. I said, 'Mamie, you feelin' all right?' And she said, 'Why honey, sure I'm all right, ain't got a pain in the world.'" Mamie never woke from that nap, just passed in her sleep.

He pointed across the street. "You see that little gray home right there? That's where I was born."

A long Louisiana road, from which you could almost see the heat rising, stretched and stretched into Angola, Louisiana. We were on our way to the penitentiary that sat on the river. A sign tacked to a tree on the road leading to the penitentiary said DO NOT DESPAIR — YOU WILL SOON BE THERE. A guard at the gate said, "Let's open the trunk, please."

He cleared us and we drove through the gate. Land spread wide. Convicts with rags tied around their heads to ward off the heat raised weed cutters to the sun and slashed at high grass along fences. Lazy cows grazed in the shade.

The warden had agreed to meet with us at 2:00. His secretary offered coffee. At 2:15, Warden Frank Blackburn came out of his office. "Come on in," he said. He sat down, a cigar in one hand, a walkie-talkie in the other. He barked an order through the walkie-talkie to one of his guards, then leaned back and swiveled around in his chair.

"Well," he said, "so you wanna know about Angola? Well, we try to run it quietly, as quietly as we can." He offered some numbers: more than four thousand inmates, more than eighteen thousand acres of land. Mostly, he said, the inmates ate what they grew.

In the fifties, sixties, and seventies the prison was known as one of the meanest in the country, inmates running wild. Then a federal judge ruled for massive reforms, and now it was widely considered a very stable penitentiary.

"You have much of a problem with escapees?"

"Not really. Of course, every now and then you'll have an inmate who breaks and runs for the river. We catch most of 'em." The warden grinned. "We bring some of 'em out of the river dead." A guard took us out to the river. Fast current, rough going for an inmate.

We rode back by the convicts cutting the grass. The guard at the gate made us open the trunk again. Stan put his feet to the pedal and we sped away from the penitentiary.

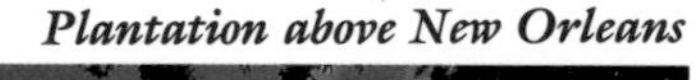
Plantation above New Orleans

New Orleans was hot and soft, its streets lined with pink-sided buildings. Kid Ory used to blow a sax here, and as a kid, Louis Armstrong sold pieces of charcoal from a cardboard box on the street.

During the Depression, representatives of plantation owners rode into town and offered men on streetcorners jobs, paying a few dollars a day to work on the sugar plantations. It was work if you could get it.

The French Quarter reeked of the nouveau riche. Satin colors swished in the night. Things were silky and rich. Palm trees cooled. There, folks ate blackened redfish, spooned gumbo, and sipped tall tropical drinks. There, jazz floated from clubs out onto the streets.

At a stoplight a tall woman, dressed in languid summer white, strolled past the car, head high, back straight as a board. Her high heels matched her dress. I thought she was headed for the clouds: a Saks Fifth Avenue woman through and through.

Years ago the red-light district in New Orleans was Storyville, but the navy had to close it down because so many of the sailors were getting venereal disease. There was still a Storyville Bar, with half-naked women dancing on a stage. But that was about all that was left from the original Storyville.

At the Old Absinthe Bar on Bourbon Street, a little marker out front said THIS IS THE BAR WHERE JEAN LAFITTE, ANDREW JACKSON, MARK TWAIN AND OTHERS WERE SERVED.

The sun set over the city, from the east, and things were full of shadows with pink and orange and rust in them.

In the quarter, the Preservation Hall Band warmed up. Folks spread out on the floor, leaned against the back brick wall, sipped drinks from paper cups. A woman at the door took the admission, two dollars, and dropped the bills into a cardboard box.

Someone said the clarinet player was just over from Paris. He wore a beret. After the lively, hour-long set, a jazzman, James Prevost, talked: "I started playing in Houma, Louisiana, back in thirty-eight and thirty-nine. First guy I worked with was a guitarist named Walter Johnson. Then, in World War II, I played with a lot of musicians in the European theater. They weren't big names, but they were good musicians."

He lit a smoke and leaned on his bass.

"I came to New Orleans in 1947. I was very well employed with a number of big bands. Stayed with one band called Four Bars for four years. Then I went out on the road. Did a lot of traveling with Roy Brown, Eddie Bo, played awhile with Fats Domino, awhile with Bill Matthews. Played with Louis once, up in Newport. It was only one day. It felt good to play with Louis."

A New Orleans night slid out under one door, morning in another.

At first you might think Willie Taylor a fool, an old man clowning around in the middle of the street, his hat at his feet for tourists to drop coins into, a Groucho Marx grin on his face. But maybe you had to be a Creole coming up in the Depression era of New Orleans to understand the grin.

French Quarter, New Orleans, Louisiana

Willie Taylor, New Orleans

Willie was seventy-one and still loved New Orleans, but he loved it more years ago. "We ain't got nothing shakin' like it shook when I was a boy," he said. They called him Soft Shoe Willie. He had been a dancer, a stand-up comic, and an extra in a few movies. "The Hollywood people come here and say, 'Get me Willie.' They know I'm New Orleans."

There was a thirty-five-cent cigar in his mouth, a few more of them in the inside pocket of his vest. He believed he could have been a star. "I never had a manager," he said, letting you in on the fatal mistake.

Manager or not, he kept dancing. "Been dancing since I was seven, all the way up to right now. People's see me dancing and they'll just scream out, *Soofft Shoooooo*."

Was a time when Willie Taylor could depend on a gig playing on one of the boats going up and down the Mississippi, but the guy who used to book him just stopped calling one day; wouldn't return Willie's phone calls either. Willie didn't sit around and mope. He decided to take his show to the streets.

As for vices, he said he never had any, steered clear of booze. "Don't like nothing but the cigar and coffee."

He'd never married. "I was a momma's boy; wouldn't leave momma for the girls. No way."

He had traveled most of the South, here and there. "Never been to Chicago or New York, though." The light in his eyes said there might be time yet. At night, when the streets can brood with danger and the unexpected, he would take the bus home, unafraid. "The Lord ain't gonna let nothin' happen to ol' Willie."

He did a little soft-shoe number. A lady nearby, who stood under the shade of her umbrella, threw her head back in laughter. There was at least ten bucks in Willie's hat.

The next morning we went to the Camilia Grill to have breakfast. It had a lovely 1940s feel. Aluminum cookware gleamed. Cool black men, dressed in white, whipped towels off their shoulders to wipe the counter clean. They slid plates down before customers and walked as if guided by jazz playing inside their heads. One of the waiters had a Clark Gable–thin mustache. Another had his hair pomaded back.

Over in a corner, a group of young women — probably freshmen or sophomores from nearby Tulane University — spun on their stools and laughed hysterically.

We ate waffles lathered with warm syrup, then left, listening to the laughter of the girls in the corner.

In the heat, New Orleans blistered full of colors and then the colors were behind us.

84

French Quarter, New Orleans

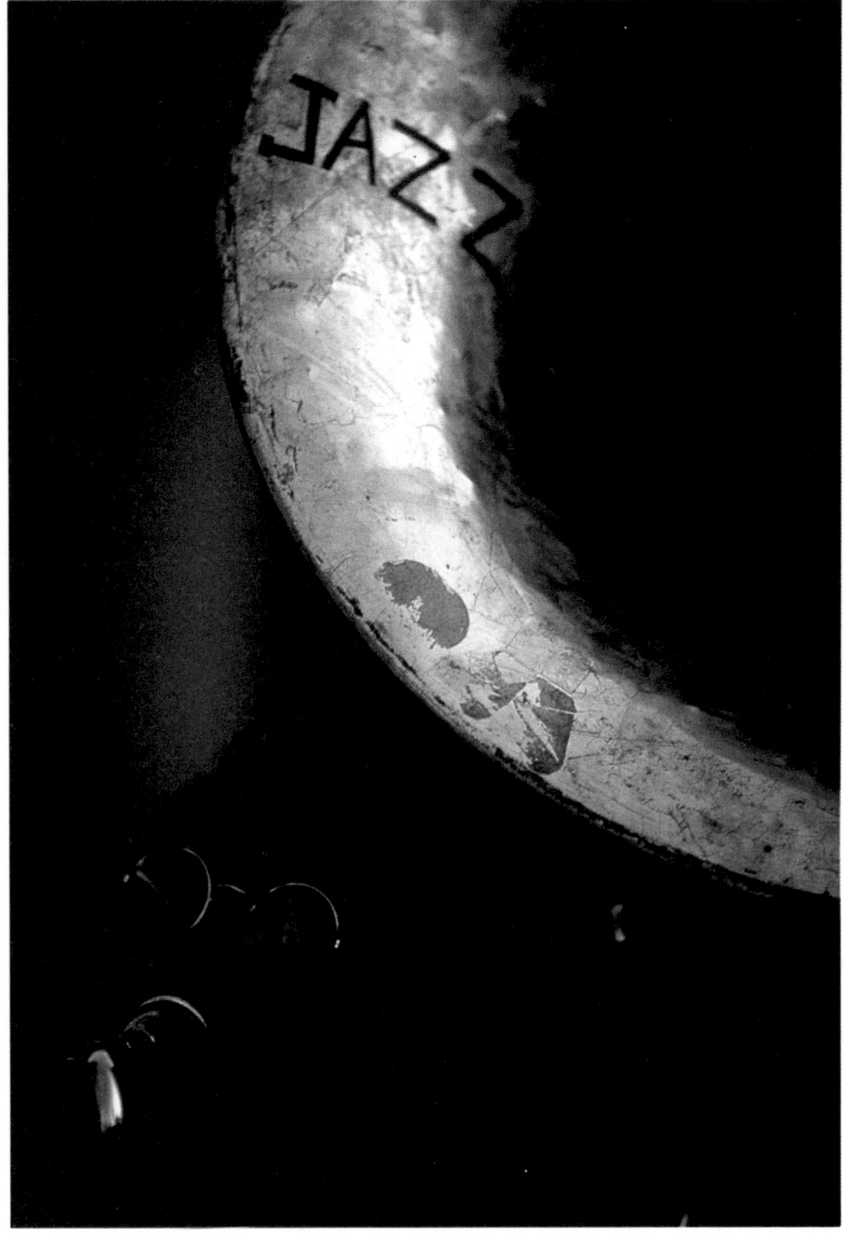

French Quarter, New Orleans

French Quarter, New Orleans

e rode a four-lane to Venice. Out the car window it was easy to see that the river was beginning to spread even wider. Venice, Louisiana, was the last piece of land in Louisiana. We chartered a small boat and started out for Pilottown, the last island before the Mississippi spilled into the Gulf of Mexico. After forty minutes we spotted land, slowed the boat, drifted into the inlet, and anchored. Quiet, still; I felt like a ghost coming back to reclaim something.

The homes on the island sat on stilts. Crawfish scampered along the muddy ground, soft on this June day. Bicycles, island transportation, were tied to railings.

River pilots sat there and waited for the big tankers to come up the Gulf of Mexico. When the tankers entered the gulf, the pilots navigated them up the Mississippi.

We walked along a railing and knocked on a screen door. A big fella named Jack Anderson came to the door.

Life had brought Jack Anderson, twenty-six, to Pilottown. Maybe it was inevitable that he would find this island, a sweet haven for river pilots. "All I ever wanted to be was a river pilot," he said. He had a maritime degree.

Only about ten families lived on the island. It used to be different. The force of nature restructured things. On August 17, 1969, Hurricane Camille kicked up off the gulf and destroyed many of the island's homes. Cows were picked up by the winds and flung out to the river, where they drowned. Rooftops were lifted from homes and went flying through the air like flying saucers. Everyone on the island ran for the community building, made of cedar wood, which the winds couldn't lift. The islanders hunkered down and prayed, and listened to their homes crack like pretzels.

When it was over, big navy boats came downriver from Baton Rouge and New Orleans to give aid and to help repair. One of the river pilots, out drifting after the storm, looked down from his boat and saw the wall clock that had hung in the island's river pilots' quarters. He picked it up, got it repaired, and now it was back where it belonged.

Some left the island as soon as they could steady themselves. A small number stayed, like Russell Staniel.

Staniel, fifty-eight, took us inside his home, which he rebuilt after the storm. "I got the stilts sixteen feet into the ground now," he said in a thick Cajun accent. He walked us through the living room, then into the kitchen, where he stood for a moment looking out the back screen door. There was nothing out there but water.

He and his wife fished shrimp. The other day they hauled in more than two hundred pounds. It was a decent way to make a

Pilottown, Louisiana

Overleaf: The Mississippi River at the Gulf of Mexico

living. He lived with only his wife. Their children cut out after high school for the big cities. He said he and his wife would never leave the island. "This is *home*."

We were able to travel by foot from one end of the island to the other along a wooden walkway. It took twenty minutes and it felt wonderful as the smell of the river and the island swam up into our nostrils. The island left one with a feeling of being far away, swept away.

A little evening wind had started up, the sun began to drop, and the green around the island suddenly seemed richer, greener. Moments passed on, and it was time for us to go. We untied the boat and drifted away, under the shade from the tall trees that leaned over the river. Russell Staniel, Jack Anderson, and a few others waved, their palms getting smaller and smaller.

When we reached the middle of the river, I looked over my shoulder to see if they were still there waving, but everyone had disappeared behind the trees that rose from the water in front of the island. Nothing moved except the trees, which swayed from the evening wind.

We stared, first at each other, then out across the water. Ripples rose, gently, as if birds were an inch under the river, flapping their wings, trying to surface. Feelings got submerged in the ripples, and are still there.

Pilottown, Louisiana